AMERICAN HISTORIC PLACES

Political and Social Movements

Ray Spangenburg and Diane K. Moser

Facts On File, Inc.

American Historic Places: *Political and Social Movements*

Facts On File, Inc.
11 Penn Plaza
New York NY 10001

Library of Congress Cataloging-in-Publication Data

Spangenburg, Ray, 1939–
Political and social movements / Ray Spangenburg and Diane K. Moser.
p. cm.—(American historic places)
Includes bibliographical references and index.
ISBN 0-8160-3404-4
1. Historic sites—United States—Juvenile literature.
2. United States—Politics and government—Juvenile literature. 3. Social movements—United States—History—Juvenile literature.
I. Moser, Diane K., 1944– . II. Title. III. Series.
E183.S75 1998
973—dc21 97-2 8096

Facts On File books are available at special discounts when purchased in bulk quantities for businesses, associations, institutions or sales promotions. Please call our Special Sales Department in New York at 212/967-8800 or 800/322-8755.

You can find Facts On File on the World Wide Web at http://www.factsonfile.com

Text design by Cathy Rincon
Cover design by Dorothy Wachtenheim
Illustrations on pages iv, 8, 20, 29, 37, 41, 54, 82, and 90 by Jeremy Eagle

Printed in the United States of America

RRD FOF 10 9 8 7 6 5 4 3 2 1

This book is printed on acid-free paper.

In dedication to

Thomas Paine,

the virtue of tolerance,

the value of dissent,

and the courage of the original American dream.

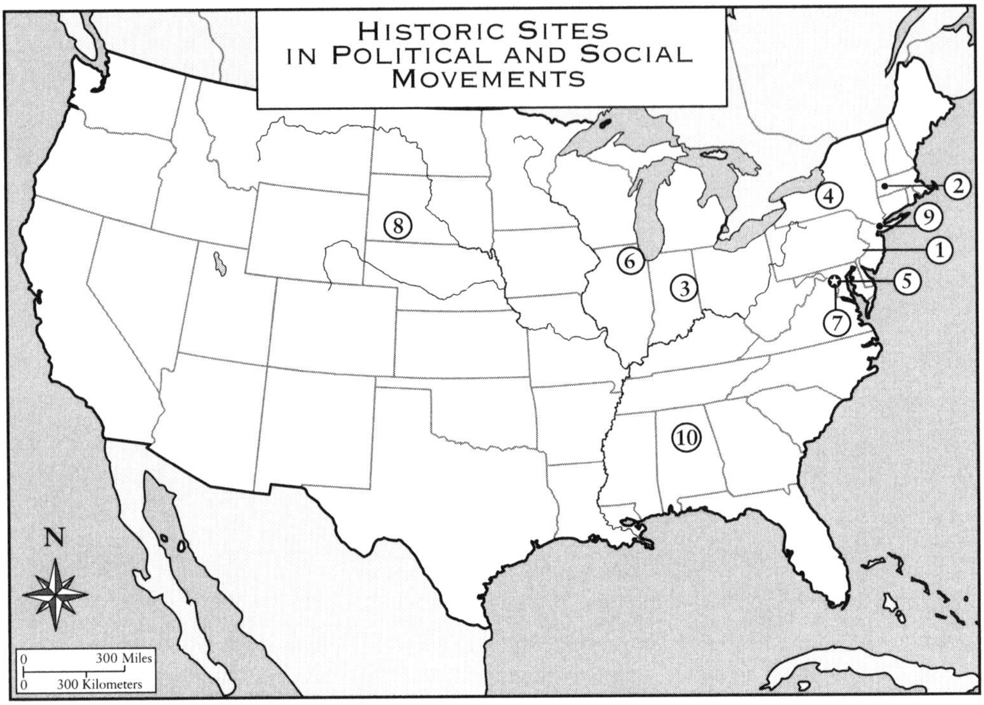

1 Valley Forge: crucible of independence

2 Hancock Shaker Village: utopian community

3 Levi Coffin House: way station on the Underground Railroad

4 Women's Rights National Historic Park: birthplace of the women's rights movement

5 Ford's Theatre National Site: site of Abraham Lincoln's assassination

6 The Jane Addams Hull-House Museum: home and first community center of social reformer Jane Addams

7 Clara Barton House: home and offices of American Red Cross founder Clara Barton

8 Wounded Knee: monument to a lost way of life

9 Ellis Island Immigration Center: gateway to America

10 The Civil Rights Movement: "...created equal," treated unequally

CONTENTS

PREFACE TO THE SERIES

History doesn't have to be dry or stuffy. And it isn't exclusively about military skirmishes and legislative proclamations—they make up only a small part of it. History is the story of life events that happened to people who cared as passionately about their lives as we care about ours. And it's the story of events that often continue to shape and influence our lives today. But getting to the human side of these stories isn't always easy. That's why there's nothing like visiting the place where an event actually occurred to get the feel of what it all meant.

The study of historic places—what happened at a particular site and how the lives of the people there were affected—has emerged as a great way to approach history, to "relive" the experience and open up to the immense diversity of American culture. Every community and region is rich in such places—places that highlight real stories about real people and events. Even if you can't actually visit such a place, the next best thing is to go there through pictures and words. Use this book and the other books in this series as jumping-off points and look around your community for places where you can experience the world of the people who once lived in your own region—and begin exploring!

♦ ♦ ♦

Each volume in this series explores a different aspect of U.S. history by focusing on a few select places. This book takes a look at historic places in the United States associated with political and social movements, from Valley Forge and the War for Independence to the South and the civil rights movement. Of course, choosing exactly which places to focus on in each book was one of the most difficult tasks of this project. We limited our choices to sites that had either been restored or maintained in authentic historic condition—most are National Historic Landmarks, chosen by the U.S. government to be preserved for their historic significance. We also tried to include examples from a wide variety of locations, events and experiences, types of sites and time periods. We then limited our selections to just a few. But many other fascinating places exist throughout the country, and that's why we mentioned other related sites at the end of some chapters (under Exploring Further) and added a list of additional sites at the back of the book (More Places to Visit).

Each chapter begins with information about the site (At a Glance). Then we explore the place—what it's like and who lived there, how the place related to that person's life and work, and what it's like to visit there today. We also look closely at one feature of the site in "A Close-Up" section, followed by a section recapping how the site came to be a protected historic site (Preserving It for the Future). A list of books and other resources concludes each chapter (Exploring Further), directing readers to either a broader or closer view of political and social movements in the United States.

Exploring historic sites not only provides a way to experience past events with fresh vividness and immediacy, it also offers a way of seeing the past through new eyes, through the eyes of those who lived it. For this adventure—and it can prove to be a lifetime adventure—this series will have accomplished its purpose if it provides the springboard for future explorations. In the words of an old Gaelic greeting, "May the wind be always at your back and may the road rise up to meet you," as you travel down these avenues of historical experience.

ACKNOWLEDGMENTS

Many people have generously helped us make this book better, and we'd especially like to thank: Mike Maione at Ford's Theatre, Saundra Jackson at Levi Coffin House, Barry Moreno at Ellis Island, Susan Finta at Clara Barton House, Sally Morse Majewski at Hancock Shaker Village, Mary Ellen Snyder at Women's Rights National Historic Park, and Mary Ann Johnson at Hull-House. At Facts On File, special thanks to our editor, Nicole Bowen, for her steady professionalism and incomparable commitment to excellence; to line editor Phil Koslow; to copy editor Katherine Barnhart; and to our former editor, James Warren, who helped us conceptualize the series.

INTRODUCTION

From the time the first humans set foot on the North American continent some 12,000 years ago, this land has become home to diverse peoples with varied backgrounds. The earliest immigrants came from Asia, across an Ice Age land bridge that formed where the Bering Strait today separates the two continents. No written record remains, of course, but scientists have found evidence that these people, like thousands of others from other continents who arrived later, came here looking for something better—better hunting and an easier, improved way of life.

Of those who came from European and Asian countries centuries later, some sought wealth, some a new start in life. Others longed for the excitement, adventure, and discovery of settling the New World, as they thought of it. Many came to America seeking freedom—religious freedom, political freedom, liberty to formulate an American Dream.

Some, in particular those who came from Africa, did not come by choice, but ultimately, they too sought freedom in America and a dream for themselves and their children.

The historical places explored in this book commemorate the struggles of those who have sought to find, reform, or widen the context of the American

Dream, those who brought to the American scene an overriding desire to establish freedoms, right social wrongs, and fight for human rights. From the soldiers who died at Valley Forge, to those who died in the 1960s in the civil rights movement and in 1973 at Wounded Knee, these people have woven the complex American fabric that we count as our heritage. They come from many countries and from many backgrounds, and history shows that the "melting pot" we call the United States has not always provided everyone with an equal welcome or with equal rights. Yet, thanks to the concept that everyone is created equal, set forth in the Declaration of Independence, political and social movements in the United States have always had more room to grow and leave a positive mark than they have had in many other countries.

George Washington's soldiers who suffered through the bitter winter of 1777–78 at Valley Forge, Pennsylvania fought to establish a new country based on the concepts of equality and liberty. The residents of Hancock Shaker Village in Massachusetts thrived in this new country, as did so many others who established utopian communities that existed outside the normal framework of society.

When the South's economic commitment to slavery threatened the nation's moral fiber, men and women like Levi and Catherine Coffin led the way to justice by hiding fugitive slaves and helping them escape to freedom through a system of secret way stations known as the Underground Railroad.

Freedom carries with it a heavy responsibility, and sometimes the outcome can be tragic. Not everyone agreed with abolitionists like the Coffins, who stood against slavery. And from 1861–65, during the presidential administration of Abraham Lincoln, the nation was torn asunder by the Civil War, which set brother against brother and friend against friend. Even when the war was concluded, some factions continued to oppose Lincoln and the victorious Unionists, and a political fanatic named John Wilkes Booth shot and killed the president. Lincoln's assassination was a sobering moment in the unfolding story of political and social movements in this country.

While African Americans struggled for emancipation from a cruel and unjust economic system that treated human beings as property to be bought and sold, women sought equality as well. Their campaign for the right to vote began at Seneca Falls, New York in 1848. One of the women's rights reformers, Elizabeth Cady Stanton, spearheaded the formation of the movement and rallied support at Seneca Falls, where today her house and the site of the 1848 convention combine with other sites to form the Women's Rights National Historic Park.

Many social movements developed, in part, from the new role women began to take as activists and reformers. One such initiative was begun by Jane Addams, who established settlement houses to help the poor in the tenement districts of Chicago in 1889. Her activism centered in her home, Hull-House, which is today a museum on the University of Chicago campus. A second movement was Clara Barton's establishment of the American Red Cross, founded to meet the emergency needs of people faced with disaster; Barton also used her home as a headquarters.

American Indians, meanwhile, were fighting a constant battle to maintain a way of life that more recent immigrants had all but obliterated. A diverse group of people composed of many separate nations, the Indians fought long and valiantly for the right to hunt buffalo on the Great Plains, gather berries in eastern Oregon and California, live in their pueblos in New Mexico and Colorado, and honor their ancestors as they had always done. But new groups were encroaching now on their hunting and burial grounds, as they themselves had occupied the lands of other tribes before them. And the two sets of cultures—Native American and immigrant—never found a way to coexist peacefully. The last battleground, at Wounded Knee, was the scene—on December 29, 1890—not of a battle but of a massacre in which U.S. troops killed some 250 Lakota (Sioux), including many women and children. After Wounded Knee, most American Indians who were not already on reservations were sent to live on one of them. In the 1970s, activists among the Indian nations began to protest the unequal treatment of their peoples. In 1973, 200 members of the American Indian Movement (AIM) occupied the village of Wounded Knee for 69 days to call attention to unjust conditions that have survived more than a century after the massacre.

By the early 20th century, thousands of immigrants were arriving each week from other lands, and the country began to fear for its stability. Was there room in the Land of Plenty for everyone who might want to come, even those who had debilitating or contagious illnesses, had criminal records, or lacked the money to get started in a new life? How wide should the welcoming arms extend? The story of the Ellis Island Immigration Center is both the story of a nation trying to protect its shores from unwanted newcomers and the story of thousands of newcomers who came and stayed and formed new, enriching patterns in the nation's fabric.

But the greatest political and social movement of the 20th century, strangely, has few well-developed historic sites that people can visit. Our final chapter explores the civil rights movement and some of its historic places, most of them bearing markers today but no interpretative programs or guides to recount their meaning. To these places we must make pilgrimages on our own, knowing their meaning in our hearts and understanding their impact in our minds. They remind us that the struggle for freedom is ongoing and that it touches the lives of us all.

In a country founded on principles of liberty, justice, and equality for all, the preservation of these historic sites is a national trust. We have fought a long, hard fight dating back 250 years or more. Those who perished at Valley Forge died for these principles. Residents of Hancock Shaker Village lived them. People like Levi and Catherine Coffin put their lives in jeopardy to defend them. Activists such as Elizabeth Cady Stanton worked to extend them. And the memory of Wounded Knee, the Montgomery Bus Boycott, and dozens of other symbols of the fight for justice serve as constant reminders of our debt to those who have risked and given their lives for these principles—the basic tenets of a nation of people who have moved here from somewhere else.

Valley Forge

CRUCIBLE OF INDEPENDENCE
Valley Forge, Pennsylvania

AT A GLANCE

Date: 1777–78

Site Where George Washington and his army spent the winter of 1777–78

Ravaged by bitter cold, hunger, and disease, the Continental Army lost many of the 12,000 soldiers who wintered here, but emerged strong and well trained for the battles ahead.

Address:
Valley Forge National Historical Park
Post Office Box 953
Valley Forge, PA 19482
(610) 783-1077

Of all the places associated with America's War for Independence, none more strongly symbolizes the suffering, sacrifice, and ultimate triumph of that struggle than Valley Forge. Thousands of American soldiers died here, even though no battle was ever fought on these grounds.

To see men without clothes to cover their nakedness, without blankets to lie upon, without shoes . . . without a house or hut to cover them until those could be built, and submitting without a murmur, is a proof of patience and obedience which in my opinion, can scarcely be paralleled.

—George Washington
at Valley Forge, December 23, 1777

♦♦♦♦♦

Modern reenactment at the soldiers' huts at Valley Forge (Courtesy Valley Forge National Historical Park)

It was a ragtag army that stumbled through the cold winter snow toward their winter encampment at Valley Forge, Pennsylvania in the freezing December weather of 1777. They were tired in body and tattered in clothing and spirit. History records that between 11,000 and 12,000 soldiers marched that winter into Valley Forge. Many of these "soldiers" were boys as young as 12 and men as old as 60. They were ill-trained and ill-equipped; marching with them were many women, most of them wives and sweethearts. The majority of the soldiers were white, but some were black, and some Native American. They had been recruited from all over the 13 colonies, and they had joined the Continental Army to fight for the liberty of those colonies, to free them from the heavy hand of Britain and to create a new nation. However, the war had not been going well for them.

Four months before, in August 1777, Sir William Howe, the general commanding British troops in North America, had landed his well-trained army of 15,000 men at the upper end of the Chesapeake Bay. Howe's strategy was to capture the city of Philadelphia, Pennsylvania, the capital of the colonies. A victory by the British troops would not only mean the capture of valuable territory but would also deal a heavy blow to the morale of the rebel colonists.

The commander in chief of the Continental Army, 45-year-old General George Washington, was determined to stop Howe at all costs. The two armies engaged in a heated battle at Brandywine Creek near Chadds Ford, Pennsylvania on September 11, 1777. Howe's strategy and forces proved superior, and the British gained the day, although Washington managed to withdraw safely with most of his men. The victorious British marched into Philadelphia on September 26, 1777, forcing the members of the Continental Congress to flee the city. But Washington was regrouping his troops. On October 4, he led his men in an attack on a contingent of Howe's forces at Germantown, several miles north of Philadelphia. In the beginning it looked as if the battle was going well for Washington's forces, but things fell apart quickly. Additional aid that Washington had been counting on failed to appear. Then a disastrous blunder occurred: Two of Washington's divisions accidentally began to fire upon each other in the thick cannon smoke and fog of the battlefield. In the confusion Howe had time to race to Germantown from Philadelphia and rally his forces—and Washington was once more forced to retreat.

With these defeats haunting him, Washington recognized that few more battles could be fought in the cold winter that was quickly closing in. And so he sought winter quarters for his army.

He selected Valley Forge, 18 miles northwest of Philadelphia, for good reasons. The area was close enough to the British so that the Americans could keep them from raiding and foraging through the interior parts of Pennsylvania, and yet it was far enough away from the main body of the British troops to prevent any surprise British attack.

Six inches of snow lay on the ground when Washington and the Continental Army arrived at their destination on December 19, 1777. The Schuylkill River, running along the camp's northern boundary, was covered with ice, and winter was coming with a fury. The march had been long and hard, and supplies had been nearly extinguished along the way. Four days after his arrival Washington had sent word to the Continental Congress of his army's condition, reporting that "2,898 men were unfit for duty because they were barefoot or otherwise naked."

On December 14, Albigence Waldo, a surgeon with Washington's army, recorded his impressions in his private diary.

> The army . . . now begins to grow sickly from the continued fatigues they have suffered this campaign. Yet they still show a spirit of Alacrity and Contentment not to be expected from so young troops. I am sick—discontented—and out of humour. Poor food—hard lodging—Cold weather—fatigue—Nasty Cloaths—nasty cookery—Vomit half my time—smoak'd out of my senses. . . . I can't endure it . . . all Confusion—smoke and cold—hunger and filthyness. . . . There comes a soldier, his bare feet are seen through his worn out shoes, his legs nearly naked from the tatter'd remains of an only pair of stockings, his Breeches not sufficient to cover his nakedness, his Shirt hanging in Strings, his hair dishevell'd, his face meagre; his whole appearance pictures a person forsaken and discouraged.

Scattered in units, called brigades, throughout the valley, the troops first lived in their flimsy and ragged tents, but by the end of December, or early January, they had constructed over 2,000 huts, each holding 12 men. Smaller huts were built for the officers, and each brigade had also been ordered to build a "hospital" measuring 15-by-25 feet for treatment of the sick. Many

This reenactment on a wintry day at Artillery Park in Valley Forge includes weaponry of the type used by Washington's soldiers. (Courtesy Valley Forge National Historical Park)

of the brigadier generals elected to move to the warmth of nearby farmhouses where they set up their headquarters, but some moved into the officers' huts to be closer to their men.

For the enlisted soldiers the huts were an improvement over their tents, but the cramped quarters, filled with unwashed men, dirty bedding, food wastes, dampness, and the constant thick smoke of the fires, soon became breeding grounds for disease.

Food, too, was scarce, and supplies were irregularly delivered. The most common staple was firecake, a completely tasteless mixture of flour and water. As Albigence Waldo recorded in his diary, " . . . a general cry thro the Camp this Evening among the Soldiers, 'No Meat! No Meat!'—the Distant vales Echo'd back the melancholy sound—'No Meat! No Meat!' Imitating the sound of Crows and Owls, also made a part of confused Musik. . . . 'What have you for dinner boys?' 'Nothing but Fire Cake and Water, Sir.' At night, 'Gentlemen the Supper is ready.' 'What is Supper Lads?' 'Fire Cake and Water, Sir.'"

By February 1, 1778, Washington reported 3,989 men "incapacitated," again ascribing the condition to lack of shoes and clothing. Sentries on guard duty were often now standing on their own hats to keep their feet from becoming frostbitten.

Men were also dying. By the end of the winter encampment, typhus, typhoid, dysentery, and pneumonia—not enemy bullets—would be the primary killers of Washington's soldiers. Over 2,000 men and boys would perish at Valley Forge.

Despite the great suffering endured by all, Valley Forge was a military encampment. If the ragtag army that had marched into the valley in December 1777 was to survive the winter and be prepared to fight again in the spring, there was much to be done. Morale and discipline had to be maintained under the trying conditions, and somehow the men, most of them inexperienced civilians, had to be toughened and trained. That job fell to one of the most impressive officers at Valley Forge, the Prussian military leader General Friedrich von Steuben.

Von Steuben had arrived at the camp on February 23, 1778, directly from France, volunteering his services and presenting a letter of introduction from Benjamin Franklin. Washington appointed him acting inspector general and ordered him to take charge of the army's training.

A tough, rigid, no-nonsense military man who had once been on the staff of Frederick the Great of Prussia, von Steuben immediately went to work. Discovering that there were not even training manuals available, von Steuben —who spoke little English—set to work writing one in French. His aides then translated the document into English and passed it on to the brigade officers.

Breaking tradition, he also directly involved himself in the men's training instead of leaving the job to his junior officers. Soon, despite all the hardships, the Continental Army was shaping up and becoming a disciplined and smartly trained fighting force.

Things were also changing outside the valley, and by the spring of 1778 the tide of war was turning dramatically. In February, France had entered into an alliance with the United States, becoming the first foreign power to recognize the infant nation. France also renounced all claims to North America east of the Mississippi River and pledged financial and military support for the United States and the Continental Army. By spring, the promised aid arrived from France, and General Howe, already in disfavor for his inability to force Washington to surrender, resigned and returned to England. Replacing him was Sir Henry Clinton, who became the new British commander in chief.

On May 6, 1778, as General von Steuben was leading the troops at Valley Forge through an all-day celebration of the new alliance with France, Clinton began evacuating the British army from Philadelphia to concentrate on New York City. At the same time, he had to send troops to the Caribbean to guard against a French threat to the British-held islands in the region.

With winter breaking up at Valley Forge, new recruits arriving daily, and much needed supplies finally appearing, the Continental Army was now ready to move. Seasoned and tempered by their long winter in the valley, their morale boosted by the knowledge of their own will for survival, and their skills sharpened by

Washington made his headquarters in this farmhouse belonging to Isaac Potts. (Courtesy Valley Forge National Historic Park)

von Steuben's drills, the Continentals were a new army as they marched forth from Valley Forge. They pursued the British through New Jersey and attacked Clinton's troops at Monmouth on June 28, 1778.

While the Battle of Monmouth would have to be called a draw, with no decisive advantage gained by either side, it was nevertheless a great moral victory for Washington's troops. The fighting would last another three years. But during that winter in the place called Valley Forge an iron spirit had been

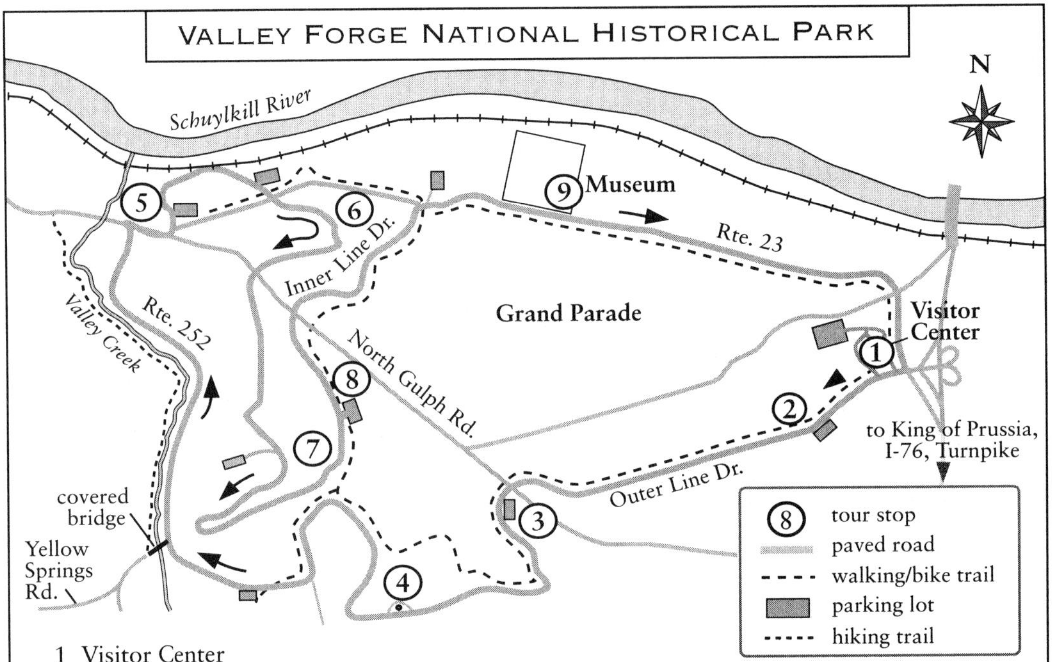

1 Visitor Center

2 Muhlenberg Brigade: reconstructed soldiers' huts

3 National Memorial Arch, a monument dedicated to those who served

4 Statue of General Anthony Wayne at the center of the area held by Pennsylvania troops under his command

5 Washington's Headquarters

6 Redoubt #4: earthen fort that anchored the north and inner defense line

7 Redoubt #3: earthen fort that anchored the south and inner defense line

8 Artillery Park, central area for artillery that was under the command of General Henry Knox

9 Museum (on privately owned grounds)

Valley Forge National Monument commemorates the winter of 1777–78, when the Continental Army established its headquarters here. Of the 11,000 troops led here by George Washington, some 2,000 were barefoot, and many suffered from the bitter cold and illness. Yet their spirit and discipline enabled them to emerge from Valley Forge ready to wage and win battles against the British.

forged, as had a will that would sustain not only the troops but the hearts of all Americans who fought for and dreamed of freedom.

Today, Valley Forge, Pennsylvania is a National Historic Park. Visitors to the 2,048-acre park can take guided tours during the summer season or obtain a self-guided tour map at the Visitor's Center that is keyed to the events of the winter of 1777–78. Points of special interest include the sparsely but authentically furnished rooms of the farmhouse of Isaac Potts, which served as General Washington's headquarters that winter, and some of the farmhouses that housed other officers. You will see reconstructed soldiers' huts, memorials, markers, and statues commemorating officers and men. You also can walk the Grand Parade area where General von Steuben trained his soldiers and visit many of the actual roads and brigade lines used by the Continental troops. Cannons still occupy many strategic points and can also be seen in Artillery Park, the original location where the weapons were stored and repaired, and where the soldiers were trained to use them. Reenactments capture the dress and spirit of the times, and the Visitor's Center houses an impressive display of firearms, swords, and accessories.

A visit to Valley Forge is an impressive reminder of an army's epic struggle to survive against terrible odds, against hunger, disease, and the unrelenting forces of nature. The site evokes echoes of the long winter suffered by the soldiers of Washington's army and of the spirit that sustained them and ultimately forged a new nation.

A CLOSE-UP: GEORGE WASHINGTON'S MARQUEE

As George Washington and his troops set out for Valley Forge in the winter of 1777, he wrote these orders: "We must make ourselves the best shelter in our power. With activity and diligence, huts may be erected that will be warm and dry. The General persuades himself that the Officers and Soldiers with one heart and one mind will resolve to surmount every difficulty with fortitude and patience becoming their profession and the sacred cause in which they are engaged. He, himself, will share in the hardships and partake of every inconvenience."

Looking back, Washington's words seem glowingly optimistic. Although he did make his headquarters in the sparsely furnished but warm home of Isaac Potts, evidence indicates that he probably slept outdoors in his marquee, or sleeping tent, as he customarily did wherever he made his headquarters. As his adopted grandson George Washington Parke Custis later recounted:

> Within [the marquee's] venerable folds, Washington was in the habit of seeking privacy and seclusion, where he could commune with himself, and where he wrote the most memorable of his dispatches in the Revolutionary War. He would remain in the retirement of the sleeping tent sometimes for hours, giving orders to the officer of his guard that he should on no account be disturbed, save on the arrival of an important express. The objects of his seclusion being accomplished, the Chief would appear at the canvas door of the marquee with dispatches in his hand, giving which to his secretary to copy and transmit, he would either mount his charger for a tour of inspection; or return to the Headquarters and enjoy social converse with his officers.

Today, visitors to Valley Forge National Historic Park can view Washington's original marquee at the Visitor's Center, thanks to a cooperative agreement with the Valley Forge Historical Society, which negotiated purchase of the marquee between 1908 and 1911 and has since maintained custodianship of this remarkable artifact of Revolutionary War history.

PRESERVING IT FOR THE FUTURE

Valley Forge was established as a National Historical Park in 1976 to preserve the historic monuments and landmarks of the winter of 1777–78.

The Valley Forge Historical Society Museum, located on private property within the park grounds, holds a collection of George Washington's possessions, as well as those belonging to soldiers of the Continental Army who wintered at Valley Forge. The collection was begun in 1908 by W. Herbert Burk, the first rector of the Washington Memorial Chapel, located next to the museum. Burk founded the all-volunteer Historical Society in 1918.

EXPLORING FURTHER

Books about Valley Forge and the Revolutionary War

Hughes, Libby. *Valley Forge*. Places in American History. New York: Dillon Press, 1993.

Kaplan, Sidney, and Emma Nogrady Kaplan. *The Black Presence in the Era of the American Revolution*. Revised ed. Boston: University of Massachusetts Press, 1989.

Kent, Deborah. *The American Revolution: Give Me Liberty or Give Me Death!* Springfield, N.J.: Enslow, 1994.

Marcus, Robert D., and David Burner. *America Firsthand. Volume 1: From Settlement to Reconstruction*. New York: St. Martin's Press, 1989.

Stein, R. Conrad. *Valley Forge*. Cornerstones of Freedom. Chicago: Children's Press, 1994.

Tuchman, Barbara. *The First Salute*. New York: Ballantine Books, 1989.

Zall, P. M., ed. *Becoming American: Young People in the American Revolution*. New York: Linnet Books, 1993.

Related Places

Memorial to the Black Soldiers of the Battle of Rhode Island
Patriots Park
Route 114 at Route 24
Portsmouth, RI 02871
(401) 683-9178

The 1st Rhode Island Regiment—the only all-African-American unit to see action in the Revolutionary War—fought here in the summer of 1778, during the Battle of Rhode Island. Brought into the Continental Army in 1777 partly because of the loss of soldiers at Valley Forge, these black soldiers fought valiantly. In a later action, at Points Bridge near Croton, New York, the entire regiment was wiped out as the men courageously attempted to protect their commander against a bayonet charge by 260 British troops.

Joseph Webb House
211 Main Street
Wethersfield, CT 06109
(860) 529-0612

In the spring of 1781, General George Washington and Count De Rochambeau met at the Joseph Webb House to plan an offensive against the British. In May 1996 murals depicting the Yorktown meeting were uncovered from beneath wall covering in the house and have been restored.

Built in 1752, this house is one of three historic 18th-century houses located at the center of old Wethersfield. The other two are the Silas Deane house, built in 1766, and the Isaac Stevens house, built in 1788. Together they form the Webb-Deane-Stevens Museum.

George Washington's Mount Vernon Estate and Gardens
South End, George Washington Parkway
Mount Vernon, VA 22121
(703) 780-2000
Internet: http://www.mountvernon.org

President Washington's elegant Georgian mansion, original outbuildings and the Washington burial site, set in 40 wooded acres. Includes gardens, a working replica of an 18th-century farm, and colonial craft demonstrations on announced weekends.

Hancock Shaker Village

UTOPIAN COMMUNITY
Pittsfield, Massachusetts

AT A GLANCE

Founded: 1790

Utopian community dating from the 18th century, founded by Shakers, refugees from religious persecution in their homelands

Established in 1790, this utopian village features 18 well-preserved buildings dating from various periods of the 18th and 19th centuries, including what may have been the first round barn in the United States.

Address:
Hancock Shaker Village
P.O. Box 927
Pittsfield, MA 01202
Telephone: (413) 443-0188 or (800) 817-1137
Fax: (413) 447-9357
Internet: http://www.hancockshakervillage.org

Hancock Shaker Village, the Shakers' "City of Peace," recalls the way of life of one of America's most successful utopian societies. Now a living history museum, the village was an active Shaker community from 1790 to 1960.

Put your hands to work and hearts to God.

—Ann Lee (1736–84)

♦♦♦♦♦

In the late 1770s, while George Washington and the Continental Army were fighting for America's independence, Ann Lee and a small group of her followers in upstate New York were engaged in their own struggle for

The round barn at Hancock Shaker Village (From the collection of Hancock Shaker Village, Pittsfield, Massachusetts)

independence. They called themselves the United Society of Believers in Christ's Second Appearing, and they wanted to renounce *all* of society and what they believed to be its inherent evils. Recently arrived from England to establish for themselves a new kingdom on earth on American soil, like many others before and after them they had been driven from their own lands by religious persecution. And like some of those others who had found refuge in America, Lee and her followers sought the promise of freedom in the New World—not only the openness of a free society, but the freedom not to take part in that society.

The uneducated daughter of a blacksmith, Ann Lee was born in Manchester, England in 1736. As a result of being forced to marry young and seeing four of her children die in childhood, she had gone through a period of deep depression, which she overcame only when she joined a religious sect called the Shaking Quakers, or Shakers (so named because of the ecstatic trembling and frenzied dancing that formed part of their worship). Sometime after joining the sect she is said to have experienced a "divine illumination" and shortly afterward began to preach a new gospel in which she opposed marriage and sexual relations, called for perfect equality between men and women, and claimed a dual nature of God—the incarnation of Jesus Christ commonly accepted by Christianity, followed by a feminine incarnation during the millennium. This incarnation she believed to be herself. After being arrested a few times in 1772 and 1773 for preaching in the streets, Lee—whose followers now called her Ann the Word, or Mother Lee—experienced another revelation. This vision instructed her to take her small group to the New World, which she did in 1774.

By the spring of 1776, while the Revolutionary War raged around them, Lee and her followers had established a small communal colony at Niskeyuna (later to be called Watervliet), New York. A charismatic speaker, Lee spent the next few years traveling through New York and New England, preaching her new gospel and recruiting new adherents to her cause. Things didn't always run smoothly, and while many people were drawn to her ideas, many others were uneasy with them. They objected particularly to her message of pacifism, which didn't sit well with those who were either caught up in the war for America's independence or had friends or relatives engaged in the conflict. In the spring of 1780, Lee and a small group of her followers were

"The Tree of Life," created by Hannah Harrison Cohoon at Hancock, 1845 (From the collection of Hancock Shaker Village, Pittsfield, Massachusetts)

arrested and briefly held on suspicion of being British sympathizers. Judged harmless and set free, Lee continued her preaching and search for converts.

Ann Lee died at Niskeyuna on September 8, 1784, nine months after the new United States Congress met at Annapolis to ratify the Treaty of Paris, marking the formal end of America's War for Independence.

With the war over, the Shaker movement Lee had started quickly began to blossom. The unsteady economy of the new nation, coupled with a rising religious revivalism, gave considerable appeal to the Shaker message of simple communal living. By the beginning of the 1830s, 19 Shaker communities had been established in New York, Massachusetts, Connecticut, New Hampshire, Maine, Ohio, Kentucky, and Indiana.

"Put your hands to work and hearts to God," Ann Lee had often said, and the Shakers followed this precept with complete devotion in all of their communities. Believing that a life of celibacy, confession, and hard labor was the only way toward total redemption, they sought to follow the rule of simplicity expressed in a well-known Shaker hymn:

"'Tis a gift to be simple, 'tis a gift to be free, 'tis a gift to come down where we ought to be. And when we find ourselves in a place just right, it will be in the valley of love and delight."

In Shaker terms, simplicity entailed as much separation as possible from the "world's people," those outside Shaker communities. To achieve this each community worked to be self-sustaining, producing all that it needed to survive and also making products and goods that could be sold to the "outside world." The proceeds would be used to buy more land or improve the quality of the Shakers' own work. Although the Shaker communities were based on spirituality, they were rich in practicality and ingenuity.

Tremendously inventive and skilled workers, the Shakers are credited with originating or improving such simple devices as the flat broom, the wooden clothespin, circular saws, metal-tipped pens, revolving ovens, round barns, and tilting chairs. Their workmanship, soon universally admired, reflected the same simplicity, honesty, and love of beauty they sought in their lifestyle. Shaker furniture, which even today is highly prized and sought after, was regarded for the simple elegance of its design and the high quality of its craftsmanship. Shaker brooms, herbs, preserves, and the packaged garden seeds that they were among the first to develop were also considered models of excellence.

Remaining separated but not isolated the Shakers were also quick to seize upon inventions of the outside world that would improve their own communities or work. In many of the areas in which their communities were located, the Shakers were among the first to have steam engines, gasoline pumps, corn shellers, lightning rods, and sewing machines. By the 1830s they had running water in their kitchens, and by the 1900s they had indoor bathrooms and telephones and were among the first to buy automobiles.

Within the Shaker communities, men and women lived and worked separately as "brothers" and "sisters" and slept in separate sides of the houses. They were forbidden to pass one another on stairways, ate at separate tables in the common dining rooms, and often entered buildings through two different front doors. But they had equal authority in the decisions governing both secular and religious life. To encourage positive relationships between the sexes and counteract any negative effects arising from enforced segregation, "union meetings" were held three or four times a week. During these gatherings small groups of men and women would sit on chairs, facing each other from a distance of a few feet. Each woman would then converse with her male counterpart, the pairs being matched on the basis of age and interests.

Initially, Shakerism's great attraction was its emphasis on an uncomplicated, agrarian life based on simple, spiritual values. But by the mid-1800s the national economy began to move away from its agricultural base, becoming more and more urban. Manufacturing gained importance in the United States as the Industrial Revolution began to take hold. And the simple, ascetic lifestyle of the Shaker religion fell further and further out of step with the rest of the country's social and economic structure. Finally, the attraction of Shakerism began to wane.

Since celibacy was at the foundation of Shaker life, the movement was dependent on new converts to keep it alive as its members aged. As early as 1874, the Shakers' dilemma became apparent when the following ad appeared in New York City newspapers: "Men, Women, and Children can find a comfortable home for life, where want never comes, with the Shakers, by embracing the true faith and living pure lives. Particulars can be learned by writing to the Shakers, Mt. Lebanon, New York." There were few takers.

Today the only active Shaker community still surviving is located at Sabbathday Lake, Maine. The Shaker heritage remains strong, however, in its legacy of accomplishments and dedication to simplicity, and although the Shakers have all but disappeared as an active religious sect their influence on American crafts and design has endured.

Visitors can experience much of that legacy firsthand at the Hancock Shaker Village, located just west of Pittsfield in western Massachusetts. The third of 19 Shaker villages established, Hancock was home to members of the Shaker society from 1790 until 1960. Today it is a living history museum, and its buildings, collections, and programs illuminate nearly three centuries of Shaker life and work.

Exploring Hancock's 20 original Shaker buildings ranging from the 1790 Laundry and Machine Shop to the 1960 Automobile Garage, you can still appreciate the emphasis on quality and the devoted simplicity of the Shaker lifestyle. Even those who might find little to relate to in the Shakers' religious message can find much to admire inside the village's 95 rooms arranged with furnishings and artifacts that were a part of the Shakers' everyday life.

The Shakers believed in simplicity, as shown by this interior view of the Elders' room. (From the collection of Hancock Shaker Village, Pittsfield, Massachusetts)

One five-story building, known simply as the Brick Dwelling, illustrates particularly well some of the unusual features of the Shaker lifestyle. Built in 1830, the building housed nearly 100 Shaker brothers and sisters, who all lived together in this structure over the following two decades. The basement contains an enormous kitchen, where visitors are likely to find an interpreter heating one of the huge ovens or baking bread, much as teams of Shaker sisters did then, working in one-month shifts to provide meals to the community. On the second floor, you can visit the two sides of the house, where the men and women lived in separate areas of the building divided by a central hallway. All the rooms in the large house—from bedrooms to infirmary—are furnished today much as they were when the building was filled with devoted Shakers going about their daily lives.

Moving back outside and wandering around the many buildings of the village, you can almost hear the Shaker hymn, "'Tis a gift to be simple, 'tis a gift to be free. . . ," as you watch modern artisans and craftspeople work on Shaker chairs, oval boxes, baskets, and brooms in the Brethren's Workshop, built around 1795. In the Sisters' Dairy and Weave Shop, constructed the same year, you can find other artisans working on rag carpets, linen towels, and other textiles.

The Round Stone Barn, built in 1826, is another stunning example of Shaker ingenuity. This is where the dairy cows were milked, arranged in a huge circle inside the barn, their heads held in frameworks called stanchions. The center of the circle contained the hay to feed the cows, and two circular walkways—one in front and one behind the cows—enabled the workers to tend the stock easily. Manure could be scooped from the barn floor and pitched through trap doors into a pit below, from which it could be accessed from the outside and carted away in wagons. Finally, a ramp on the outside enabled the Shakers to roll wagonloads of hay up to the second level, from which it could be pitched into the central area for feeding.

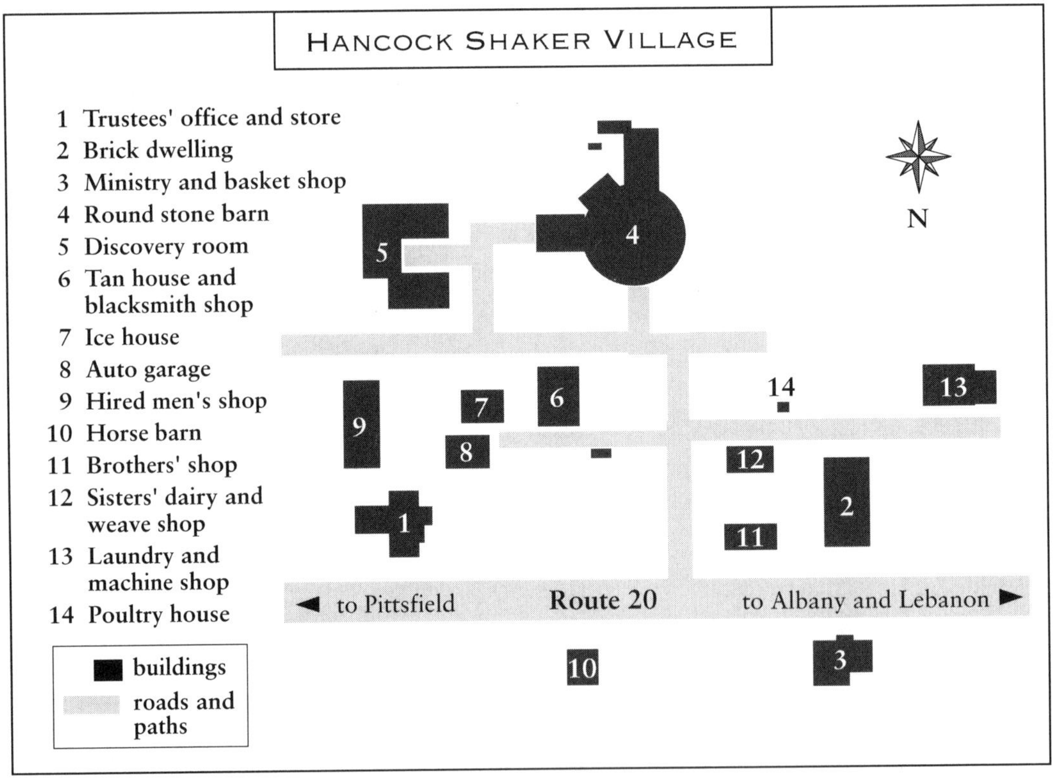

Partial map of the Shakers' village at Hancock, based on the 1945 Historic Building Survey. Additional buildings have been restored since then—such as the meeting house, the schoolhouse, and the privy—and a visitors' center was added in 1972. Buildings removed by the Shakers in the 20th century have been omitted.

Farming was a major part of all Shaker communities, and today the Hancock Shaker Village still raises a variety of the historic breeds of livestock once found on the typical Shaker farm—including shorthorn cattle, merino sheep, and silver-laced wyandotte and dominique chickens. The farm staff still uses oxen and period equipment to work the farmland and gardens.

A farming community in the 1830s required leather goods—harnesses for the teams of oxen and horses, shoes for the brethren and sisters, and hats. The Shakers produced their own leather in the Tanning House, built in 1835. By the 1870s, the lower floor provided space for the work of the community blacksmith at his forge and a cider press that made juice and drink from the orchard fruits. The second floor of the Tanning House, however, was devoted to the crafts for which the Shakers are most famous: woodworking and cabinetry. Today, you can still see a smithy working here at his forge, and cabinetmakers milling chair legs and fashioning tables, as if you had stepped back in time to the 19th century.

For all its splendid work facilities, the essence of the Hancock village was above all spiritual, and that essence can still be felt inside the Meetinghouse. Most Shaker meetinghouses were built on the same plan, designed in the 1780s by Moses Johnson, a Shaker brother from Harvard, Massachusetts. The meetinghouse at Hancock Shaker Village today is not the original Hancock Meetinghouse—that one was torn down in 1938. But because it was built using Johnson's design, it looks just like the original, even though it was moved here from another community in 1962.

Balance and simplicity are the key elements in the design, with separate doors for men and women opening into a plain, unadorned room with plank flooring and wooden benches. Here the Shakers held their Sunday worship services, with men and women seated in separate areas of the room. When visitors came from the "outside," they were seated on benches around the edge of the room, where they might hear the worshipers give impassioned, emotional testimonials of faith. Or, having pushed the benches aside, the worshipers would move vigorously about the room in the characteristic dances and songs that were unique to their form of worship.

You can almost hear the Shaker hymn echo, "And when we find ourselves in a place just right, it will be in the valley of love and delight . . . ," and perhaps here in Hancock, for many years, the Shakers truly found such a place.

A CLOSE-UP: EXPERIENCING THE SHAKER WAY OF LIFE

In the 1910 Barn Complex, visitors of all ages can try on replicas of traditional Shaker clothing, including bonnets, cloaks, smocks, dresses, and hats of felt or straw. Open during the summer, the Discovery Room located here provides visitors with opportunities to card, spin, and weave wool; learn basket-making techniques; or write with a quill pen.

Farming was the backbone of all Shaker communities, and the Shakers raised livestock, cultivated crops, and tended orchards and gardens to maintain their self-sufficiency. Visitors can still see these activities in progress today, much the same as in the 19th century. In the summer, staff members give talks about the role of farm animals in village life. They also discuss how the historic breeds are different from common breeds today.

Herb gardens also played an important role in Shaker agriculture, supplying plants for their own home remedies as well as for the pharmaceutical industry of the "outside world." In 1873 the Shakers published the *Druggists' Handbook of Pure Botanic Preparations*, in which more than 300 varieties of plants are mentioned. Hancock's specimen herb garden today contains 90 varieties.

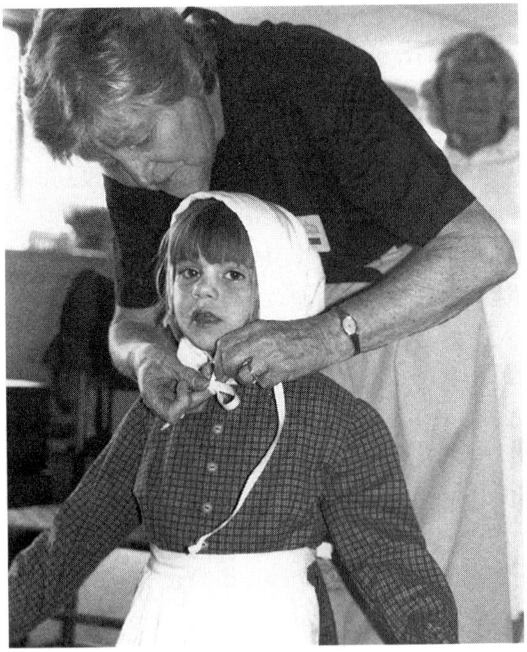

In the Discovery Room, located in the Barn Complex, visitors can try on Shaker clothing and experience a little of what life was like in Hancock in the 19th century. (From the collection of Hancock Shaker Village, Pittsfield, Massachusetts)

In addition there are two heirloom vegetable gardens; one contains plant varieties included on Shaker seed lists from the 1830s, and the other from the 1890s. The cultivation techniques used in Hancock's garden are typically Shaker, as documented in the Shakers' 1843 gardening manual, and represent what we would today call organic gardening. The village's gardeners gather and save seeds from the plants, and the museum shares them through the international Seed Savers' Exchange to help perpetuate unusual or endangered varieties of 19th-century vegetables.

PRESERVING IT FOR THE FUTURE

Hancock Shaker Village, located on 1,200 acres in the Berkshire Hills of western Massachusetts, was an active community from 1790 to 1960, when it became an outdoor history museum of Shaker life. Today its buildings, collections, and programs interpret three centuries of Shaker life and work.

EXPLORING FURTHER

Books about the Shakers

Bial, Raymond. *Shaker Home*. Boston: Houghton Mifflin, 1994.

Bolick, Nancy O'Keefe, and Sallie G. Randolph. *Shaker Villages*. New York: Walker & Co., 1993.

Brewer, Priscilla J. *Shaker Communities, Shaker Lives*. Paperback ed. Hanover, N.H.: University Press of New England, 1988.

Burns, Deborah E. *Shaker Cities of Peace, Love, and Union: A History of the Hancock Bishopric*. Hanover, N.H.: University Press of New England, 1993.

Spriggs, June. *By Shaker Hands: The Art and World of the Shakers*. Hanover, N.H.: University Press of New England, 1990.

Thorne-Thomsen, Kathleen. *Shaker Children: True Stories and Crafts*. Chicago: Chicago Review Press, 1996.

Turner, Ann Warren. *Shaker Hearts*. New York: HarperCollins, 1997.

Williams, Jean K. *The Shakers*. Danbury, Conn.: Franklin Watts, 1997.

Related Places

Canterbury Shaker Village
Canterbury, NH 03224
(603) 783-9511
Internet: http://www.shakers.org

Canterbury Shaker Village, the sixth of 19 Shaker communities, was founded in the 1780s. At its peak in 1860, some 300 people lived, worked, and worshiped in 100 buildings on 4,000 acres and made their living from farming, selling seeds and herbs, manufacturing medicines, and making crafts.

The Shaker Museum
United Society of Shakers
Sabbathday Lake
Poland Spring, ME 04274
(207) 926-4597
Internet: http://www.shakerworkshops.com/sdl.htm

Sabbathday Lake, established in 1794 as "Chosen Land," is the only Shaker community that continues to be active today. It contains 18 well-maintained buildings. Visitors are welcome here, and the site features a museum, Shaker store, and library. Exhibits include Shaker furniture, tin and woodenware, folk art, textiles, early American tools, and farm implements. Guided tours and special programs are available.

Shakertown at Pleasant Hill
(Pleasantville Historic District)
3500 Lexington Road
Harrodsburg, KY 40330
(606) 734-5411 or (800) 734-5611
Internet: http://www.tourky.com/shakervillage/info.html

Built in the 1800s, this was the most successful of the 19th-century communitarian settlements. It is typical of the closed groups established by Shakers to create independent utopian colonies. By 1820 some 500 Shakers lived here on 3,000 acres, but the community was dissolved in 1910.

Levi Coffin House

WAY STATION ON THE UNDERGROUND RAILROAD
Fountain City, Indiana

AT A GLANCE

Built: 1839

Home of Levi and Catharine Coffin, 1839–ca.1846

This eight-room Federal-style house in Indiana became a hub of the Underground Railroad in several surrounding states. The restored Coffin House is open to visitors, who can see the hidden quarters for runaway slaves and witness the past brought to life by historical interpreters.

Address:
Levi Coffin House
113 U.S. 27N
Fountain City, IN 47341
(765) 847-2432

Called the president of the Underground Railroad and an important figure in the abolitionist movement, Levi Coffin moved to Indiana in 1826, began a business, and opened his house as a depot for escaped slaves. In their 20 years here he and Catharine Coffin helped about 2,000 men, women, and children escape to freedom. The Coffins later moved to Cincinnati, Ohio where they helped about 1,100 more fugitives.

Children, if you are tired, keep going; if you are scared, keep going; if you are hungry, keep going; if you want to taste freedom, keep going.

—Harriet Tubman,
former slave and conductor
on the Underground Railroad

♦♦♦♦♦

Levi and Catharine Coffin's home in Indiana offered a hiding place for escaped slaves from 1839 to 1847, when the Quaker couple moved to Cincinnati to continue their Underground Railroad operation from an Ohio base. (Courtesy of the Levi Coffin State Historic Site)

Escaping to freedom was a dangerous undertaking for any slave living in the South in the years before the Civil War, and increasingly stringent legislation, such as the Fugitive Slave Act of 1850, made it more and more difficult. Setting out by night, often with nothing but the clothes they were wearing, most had only the North Star to guide them. They could travel just a few miles each night, ever ready to duck out of sight if a search party came along. Slave owners were deadly serious about recapturing escaped slaves. They believed they were in the right, and they had power and the law on their side.

If fugitives could find their way to the homes of antislavery supporters, though, they could be assured of a safe hiding place. There they would also usually be given the names of others who would help, as well as places to go for food, shelter, and even aid in transportation. The chain of stops on the path to freedom became known as the Underground Railroad, although there were no trains or tracks, just a loosely organized network of people and safe

The entrance to the secret hiding place in the garret of the Coffin house (Courtesy of the Levi Coffin State Historic Site)

houses. The system was secretly coordinated to help escaping slaves make their way across the South to the northern states, Canada, and freedom. The abolitionist homes were known as stations or way stations. The adjective *underground* arose from the secrecy required for the safe operation of the system.

For thousands of escaped slaves, an eight-room Federal-style brick home in Newport (now Fountain City), Indiana became an important haven on their journey to Canada. It was the home of Levi and Catharine Coffin.

A white Quaker who left North Carolina in protest against the ever-increasing severity of the Black Codes, Levi Coffin and his wife Catharine arrived in Newport in 1826. There, they established a store in the village, selling foodstuffs, hardware, and most anything else the villagers might need. The Coffins were disturbed when they realized that, while Newport was settled primarily by antislavery Quakers, none of their neighbors seemed to be doing anything to further the cause of abolitionism. As one historian has put it, the Newport Quakers rejected slavery rather than opposing it.

Nearby, however, the Coffins found an active Underground Railroad operation led by freed slaves, who were themselves in constant danger of being kidnapped and illegally resold into bondage. The Coffins committed themselves to the cause. They invited their white neighbors to meet in their home with black runaways and the local black Underground Railroad conductors. Soon afterward, the Coffin house became a hub in the vast Underground Railroad network for several surrounding states.

In their flight through this region, slaves used three main routes to cross into freedom: through Madison or Jeffersonville in Indiana or Cincinnati in Ohio. From these points, the fugitives were taken to Newport. Common signals that the coast was clear were a smoking chimney and a quilt hanging in the backyard. When hunting parties were in hot pursuit, the route was changed to lose them.

Once runaway slaves arrived at the Coffin house, they might be concealed for several weeks, until they gained enough strength to continue their journey. The Coffin sanctuary was enormously successful: Not a single slave who arrived safely in Newport failed to reach freedom. Once they entered the Coffins' domain, they were lost to the slave catchers.

A visit to the house gives fascinating insight into ingenious methods born of necessity. In the barn visitors can see a wagon equipped with a false bottom

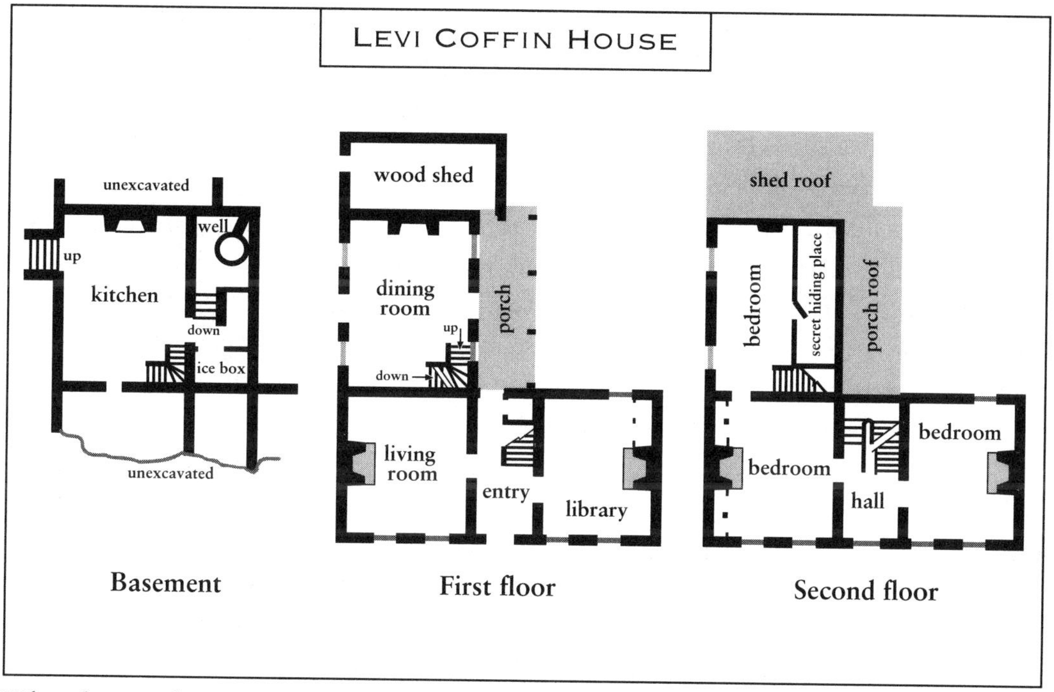

When slave catchers were in town, fugitives sheltered by the Coffins could slip up the stairway from the dining room to the second-floor bedroom, where a hidden room offered safety until the danger passed.

that slid back to provide a hidden compartment for safe transportation. They can also see where the innovative Coffins built a secret door from the hired girl's room into a hidden garret, where their fugitive guests could be safe. A back stairway led from the dining room, up to the hired girl's room, for quick access. Interpreters dressed in period clothing evoke the reality of the Coffins' lives and those of the fugitives who stayed there.

Unlike most participants in the Underground Railroad, Levi Coffin was open and direct in his opposition to the Fugitive Slave laws. And although he was a member of a clandestine operation, he was not hesitant to confront slave hunters. He used Indiana laws on search warrants and illegal seizure to keep slave hunting parties at bay. And he did not hesitate to prosecute them if they stepped out of line. As a result, Coffin kept his house from ever being searched, even though he and his wife were openly helping fugitives.

Levi Coffin was also active in helping to organize antislavery societies and was always willing to work with anyone to help a slave obtain freedom.

Antislavery society meetings were often raided by slavery sympathizers, who sometimes threw stones at the abolitionists. As a consequence, the Indiana yearly meeting of Friends (Quakers), who stood staunchly against any show of violence, ruled that Friends' meetinghouses could not be used for abolitionist gatherings—a ruling that threatened to divide the Quakers.

Coffin not only worked to help fugitive slaves but was also active in establishing and supporting two schools to promote literacy. He also joined other abolitionists in opposing the use of goods produced through the use of slavery. The position had an economic consequence—goods produced by free labor were almost always more expensive. But many abolitionists were willing to pay the price for "Free Labor Goods," as they were called. Coffin carried Free Labor Goods in his store, which soon became one of the largest Midwest outlets for these products. The leaders of the movement for Free Labor Goods bought cotton in Mississippi communities where small farmers did not have slaves. They also made sure that the cotton was ginned and transported to the distribution center in Philadelphia without the use of slave labor. Then materials were woven and shipped to the Midwest. The movement used similar procedures for salt, sugar, and as many other commodities as possible. In 1847, Levi and Catharine Coffin moved their Free Labor Goods operation to Cincinnati, where they continued their work with the Underground Railroad, helping 1,100 additional fugitives from their Ohio home.

Throughout his work in the Underground Railroad and the Free Labor Goods movement, Levi Coffin gained wide respect and established lasting friendships. In the years following the Civil War, even former slaveowners who had heard Coffin talk openly about the evils of slavery often asked him to help see that the emancipated slave children received an education in the North and got established well. Catharine Coffin always worked with Levi on these causes and backed him completely—theirs was a team operation, and she never faltered, even though the Coffins' unflinching involvement in the cause of abolition brought many hardships.

A CLOSE-UP: BASEMENT KITCHEN AND SPRING ROOM

One of the unusual features of the Coffin house is the basement kitchen and the spring room located to the south under the porch. During restoration, a 2-inch layer of sand was found under the concrete slab floor that had been added when the room was modified to serve as a furnace room. Beneath the sand, restorers found the original brick floor. This had once been the kitchen floor.

Water was easily drawn from an open well located in the spring room in the basement of the house.
(Courtesy of the Levi Coffin State Historic Site)

In the adjacent spring room area, removal of the concrete revealed brick rubble, dirt, and sawdust. The west end of this area turned out to be 6 inches below the kitchen floor, and a moist clay slope led to a second level 5 feet lower. In the center of this area was a circular well 5 feet deep with the brick wall still in place. Workers clearing out the well were delighted to see it immediately fill with water. Judging by the holes in the walls, there had once been a deck suspended above the well, probably used to store stone jars containing pickled foods or canned goods. No doubt the Coffins also hung hams and bacon in this cool spot.

The presence of sawdust indicates that this area was used for storing ice as well. Typically ice was cut from the mill ponds during the winter, then stored under sawdust for use when the weather warmed.

From the kitchen, a stairway winds up to the dining room and from there a second stairway winds to the second story of the house to the hired girl's room. There, a small bed could be moved aside to reveal the hidden door to the attic area where fugitives hid.

PRESERVING IT FOR THE FUTURE

In 1910, the Coffin House was converted to a rural hotel. However, much of the materials removed from the house were stored safely in the attic. The Coffin house was purchased in 1967 by the state of Indiana and is now a State Historic Site, part of the Indiana State Museum and Historic Sites Division of the Department of Natural Resources. The house was restored with care and attention to historic accuracy, furnished with period pieces, and then opened to the public in 1970. Levi Coffin House is a registered National Historic Landmark and is operated by the Levi Coffin House Association.

EXPLORING FURTHER

Books about Levi Coffin and the Underground Railroad

Bentley, Judith. *"Dear Friend": Thomas Garrett & William Still: Collaborators on the Underground Railroad.* New York: Cobblehill, 1997.

Blockson, Charles L. *The Underground Railroad.* New York: Prentice-Hall, 1987.

Buckmaster, Henrietta. *Let My People Go: The Story of the Underground Railroad and the Growth of the Abolition Movement.* Southern Classics Series. Columbia, S.C.: University of South Carolina Press, 1992.

Campbell, Stanley W. *The Slave Catchers: Enforcement of the Fugitive Slave Law, 1850–1860*. Chapel Hill: University of North Carolina Press, 1968.

Gara, Larry. *The Liberty Line: The Legend of the Underground Railroad*. Lexington, Ky.: University Press of Kentucky, 1996.

Ludwig, Charles. *Levi Coffin and the Underground Railroad*. New York: Herald Press, 1975.

Rappaport, Doreen. *Escape from Slavery: Five Journeys to Freedom*. New York: HarperCollins Juvenile Books, 1991.

Taylor, M. W. *Harriet Tubman: Antislavery Activist*. New York: Chelsea House Publishers, 1991.

Related Places

Harriet Tubman House
180 South Street
Auburn, NY 13021
(315) 252-2081

The house of Underground Railroad conductor Harriet Tubman from 1857 to 1913 served as a home for aged and indigent blacks from 1908 to 1914. Tubman purchased the modest two-story frame house with the assistance of the abolitionist and politician William H. Seward, later secretary of state in President Abraham Lincoln's administration.

Seward House
33 South Street
Auburn, NY 13021
(315) 252-1283

Home of William Henry and Frances Seward. The Seward house was also an Underground Railroad stop, hiding fugitives in a large storage area above the carriage house, which was connected to the main house. In addition to many other items of historical interest, artifacts connected with Seward's neighbor and fellow Underground Railroad conductor Harriet Tubman are on display.

John Rankin House State Memorial
1824 Liberty Hall
Ripley, OH 45167
(937) 392-1627 or (800) 752-2705
Internet: http://winslo.state.oh.us/ohswww/places/rankin

The first stop across the Ohio River on the way from Tennessee to freedom in Canada, Rev. John Rankin's house provided a haven for those evading the slave catchers patrolling the river. Rankin and his wife, Jean, founded the American Anti-Slavery Society here in 1828 and helped approximately 2,000 individuals flee the bonds of slavery. Visitors can tour the home, which includes a cellar beneath the barn and a hiding place in the attic, both used to conceal fugitives.

Women's Rights National Historic Park

BIRTHPLACE OF THE WOMEN'S RIGHTS MOVEMENT
Seneca Falls, New York

AT A GLANCE

Built: Wesleyan Chapel, 1843; Stanton house, 1846

Park encompassing numerous historic sites related to establishment of a national movement for women's rights

Site of the first Women's Rights Convention, held in 1848. Nearby, visitors can tour the residence of Elizabeth Cady Stanton, the poet, philosopher, and leader of the women's rights movement who delivered the call for women's suffrage at the Seneca Falls Convention of 1848.

Address:
Women's Rights National Historic Park
Visitor Center
136 Fall Street
Seneca Falls, New York 13148
(315) 568-2991
Internet: http://www.nps.gov/wori/
http://www.rochester.edu/SBA/park.htm

Women's Rights National Historic Park was established by an act of Congress in 1980. The Historic District consists of the restored home of Elizabeth Cady Stanton, the Wesleyan Chapel, Declaration Park with its 140-foot waterwall, and the park Visitor Center.

Resolved, that it is the duty of the women in this country to secure themselves their sacred right to the elective franchise.

—Declaration of Sentiments, read to the convention by Elizabeth Cady Stanton, 1848

♦♦♦♦♦

Certainly in the mid-1800s one of the most controversial issues to be voiced in public, and in private as well, was that of women's rights. By law or social custom, women were denied not only the right to vote but in most cases the right to attend college, hold office, or earn a living outside such "accepted" positions as teacher, seamstress, domestic, or millworker. Married women could not make contracts, sue in court, divorce abusive husbands, gain custody of their children, or own property—not even their own clothes.

Elizabeth Cady Stanton's house in Seneca Falls (Courtesy of the National Park Service)

It was in the Wesleyan Chapel, in Seneca Falls in 1848, that determined women came together on a large scale for the first time to pro-

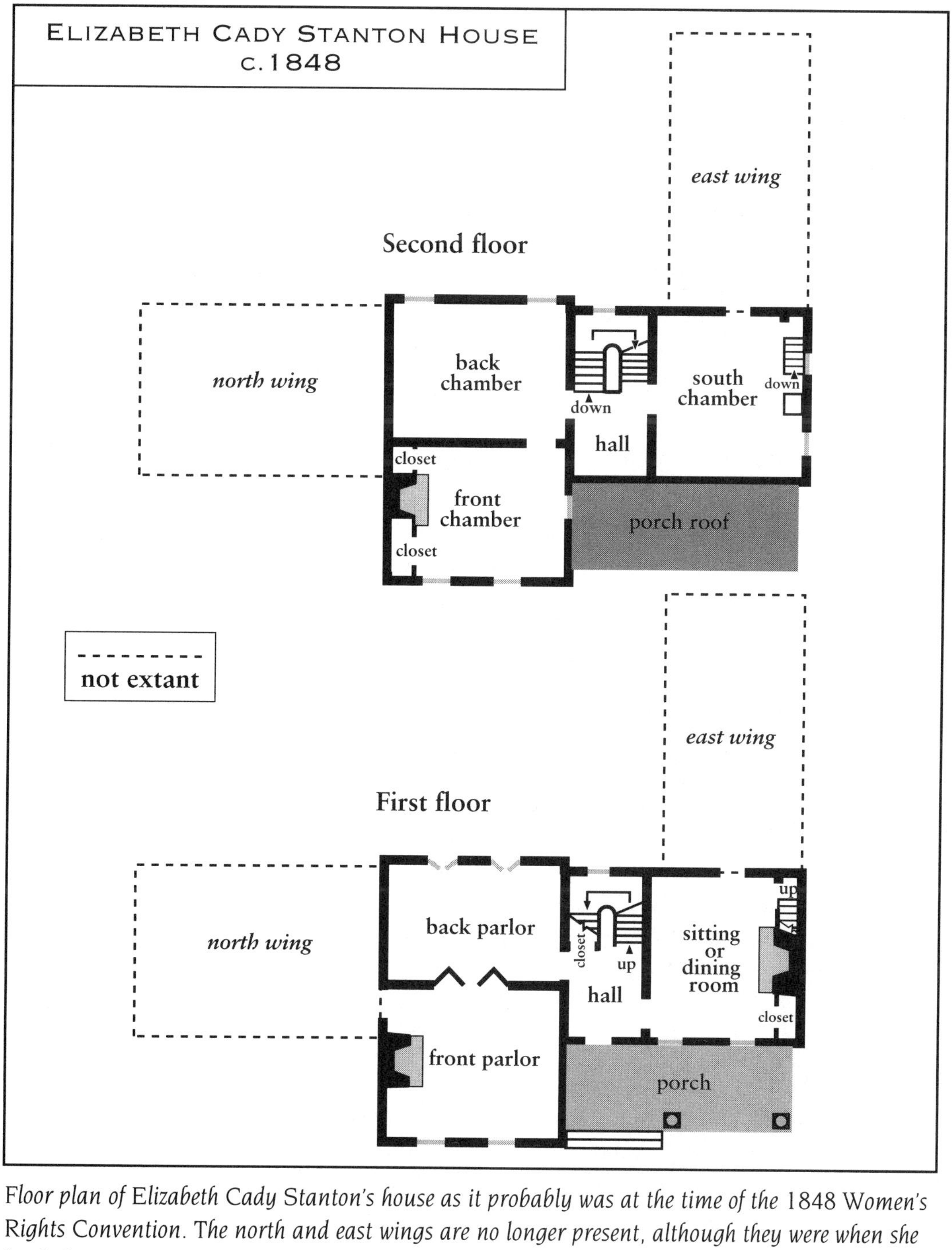

Floor plan of Elizabeth Cady Stanton's house as it probably was at the time of the 1848 Women's Rights Convention. The north and east wings are no longer present, although they were when she lived there.

test those unfair restrictions in the first Women's Rights Convention held in the United States.

Organized by Stanton, Lucretia Mott, and others, the convention was the beginning of the women's rights movement in America. As Elizabeth Cady Stanton declared on July 19 in Seneca Falls:

> The right is ours. Have it, we must. Use it, we will. The pens, the tongues, the fortunes, the indomitable wills of many women are already pledged to secure this right. The great truth that no just government can be formed without the consent of the governed we shall echo and re-echo in the ears of the unjust judge, until by continual coming we shall weary him.

Certainly when Stanton (1815–1902) moved to this upstate New York town at the age of 31 with her husband and children, the setting did not strike her as a likely locale for such a historic gathering of crusaders. In fact, the contrast with her former home in Boston, Massachusetts left her feeling stifled, unimpressed, and disappointed with her new surroundings. Writing later in her reminiscences, she noted:

> In Seneca Falls my life was comparatively solitary, and the change from Boston was somewhat depressing. There, all my immediate friends were reformers, I had near neighbors, a new home with all the modern conveniences, and well-trained servants. Here our residence was on the outskirts of the town, roads very often muddy and no sidewalks most of the way. Mr. Stanton was frequently from home, I had poor servants and an increasing number of children . . . the novelty of housekeeping had passed away, and much that was attractive in domestic life was now irksome. I had so many cares that the company I needed for intellectual stimulus was a trial rather than a pleasure.

Today a life-size bronze statue of Elizabeth Cady Stanton, joined by similar statues of Lucretia Mott, Jane Hunt, and other early leaders of the fight waged by American women for equal rights, stands proudly in place at the National Historic Park Visitor Center in Seneca Falls. It is a reminder that here, in this quiet town in west central New York, Stanton did find time not only for intellectual stimulation but to join with others in laying the foundation for the women's rights movement.

Although decidedly not Boston, Seneca Falls in the mid-1800s was far from being an isolated little village. A stopover on the Great Western Turnpike, it was also connected by a feeder line to the then bustling Erie Canal System. Passenger rail service arrived in 1841, and as a result of Seneca's three major travel connections—road, canal, and rail—new arrivals were constantly coming and going through the town. Many decided to stay, at least for a while, bringing in a constantly refreshing source of news, information, and new ideas. The village had also become a home to two major social reformist groups, the Hicksite Quakers and Wesleyan Methodists, who had broken with their parent churches over the issue of slavery. The Methodists built the Wesleyan Chapel in Seneca Falls, which quickly became a busy center for often heated discussions of slavery and other controversial social and political issues. It also was destined to be the pulpit for the first convention on women's rights.

Stanton first formed an alliance with Lucretia Mott in 1840, when they met while attending an international antislavery conference in London. Stanton was there with her husband, the abolitionist William Brewster Stanton, whom she had married that same year. She and Mott became angered when they and the other women attending were denied official participation in the conference. The two became determined to devote their considerable energy to the cause of women's rights.

Ironically, years later Stanton would refuse to support the 15th Amendment, which extended suffrage to African-American males, on the grounds that women (of all races) were still being denied the right to vote. While her argument was understandable enough, she made unfortunate public comments about black males (in addition to unfortunate phrases describing Irish and other "foreign" males), and her remarks became an embarrassment to the struggling women's rights movement.

The 1848 convention in Seneca Falls, though, marked a decided breakthrough for the movement. Here, on July 19 and 20, 68 women and 32 men passed a Declaration of Sentiments (also known as the Seneca Falls Declaration), which closely paralleled the Declaration of Independence of 1776. It listed 16 forms of discrimination against women and denounced inequities in property rights, education, employment, religion, marriage, family, and suffrage. The last, the demand for the "elective franchise"—the right of women to vote—was so controversial, even among those attending the convention, that it passed only by the narrowest of margins and over the objections of Mott.

"We hold these truths to be self-evident that all men and women are created equal . . . ," are the words you can find today engraved on a fountain near the Wesleyan Chapel in Seneca Falls. Such reminders are everywhere in this small village. Portions of the chapel still stand, the site where 300 women and men (including reformists, locals, and the curious) gathered in 1848 to hear the first-ever formal demands for women's rights.

Since that time, the building was enlarged and went through many transformations, serving as a movie theater, furniture store, roller rink, auto repair shop, car dealership, and laundromat. Later additions have been stripped back to expose today the original historic structure, including the east and west walls and the roof.

Nearby, the National Historic Park Visitor Center features not only the impressive collection of life-size bronze statues mentioned above but also a maze of colorful interactive exhibits as well as featured talks and a short film detailing the history of women in the United States. The National Women's Hall of Fame, at 76 Fall Street in Seneca Falls, outlines the many contributions of women to society, including the accomplishments of such notables as Susan B. Anthony, Sojourner Truth, Amelia Earhart, Barbara McClintock, and many others. New names and exhibits are added regularly, and telephones next to the colorful exhibits allow visitors to hear the words of many famous women.

Outside again, on the grounds of Declaration Park, you can visit an impressive 140-foot waterwall on which is inscribed the Declaration of Sentiments, along with the names of its 100 signers.

Not far away, you can tour the Elizabeth Cady Stanton House, Stanton's home during the 15 years she spent in Seneca Falls (1847–62). Guided tours and talks by park rangers bring Stanton's days in Seneca Falls to life and allow a glimpse of what it must have been like in those exciting times filled with visits and strategy sessions with such famous

Opposite: *Exhibits in the towns of Waterloo and Seneca Falls in upstate New York commemorate the Women's Rights Convention of 1848 and the activists—including Lucretia Mott, Elizabeth Cady Stanton, Mary Ann and Thomas M'Clintock, and others—who worked to bring about the birth of women's rights in the United States.*

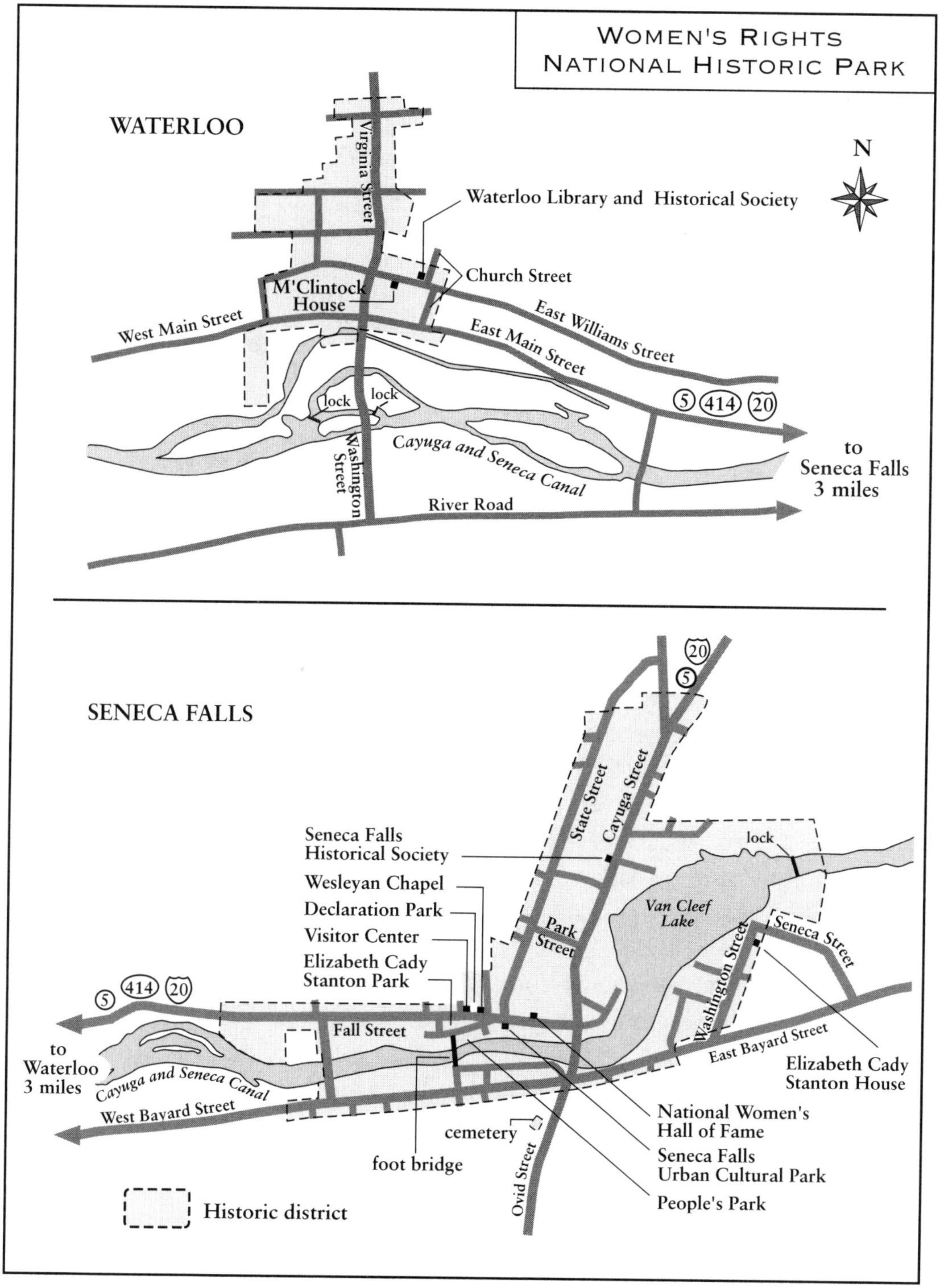

WOMEN'S RIGHTS NATIONAL HISTORIC PARK
WATERLOO
N
Virginia Street
Waterloo Library and Historical Society
Church Street
M'Clintock House
West Main Street
East Williams Street
East Main Street
lock
lock
5 414 20
Washington Street
Cayuga and Seneca Canal
to Seneca Falls 3 miles
River Road
SENECA FALLS
20
5
State Street
Cayuga Street
Seneca Falls Historical Society
lock
Wesleyan Chapel
Declaration Park
Visitor Center
Elizabeth Cady Stanton Park
Van Cleef Lake
Park Street
Seneca Street
Washington Street
5 414 20
to Waterloo 3 miles
Fall Street
Cayuga and Seneca Canal
West Bayard Street
East Bayard Street
Elizabeth Cady Stanton House
National Women's Hall of Fame
Seneca Falls Urban Cultural Park
People's Park
cemetery
foot bridge
Ovid Street
Historic district

allies as Mott, Anthony, Frederick Douglass, and many others.

Traveling to the nearby area of Waterloo, you can also pass by the historic Hunt House (now privately owned), home of the Quakers Jane and Richard Hunt, where many of the plans for the Seneca Falls Convention were discussed. Also in Waterloo, on East Williams Street, visitors can tour the M'Clintock House, home of reformists Mary Ann and Thomas M'Clintock. In this house, the Declaration of Sentiments was first drafted.

Plans for the 1848 Women's Rights Convention were laid at the M'Clintock's house, which is located in nearby Waterloo and is also open to the public as part of the Women's Rights National Historic Park. (Courtesy of the National Park Service)

The Seneca Falls Historical Society, housed not far from the Wesleyan Chapel, holds an impressive display of mementos and artifacts from the days of the convention. Here, visitors can see the restored rocker of Elizabeth Cady Stanton as well as the drop-leaf desk where she wrote many of the speeches she prepared for Susan B. Anthony. Anthony's black velvet cape can also be seen, as well as many handwritten speeches by Amelia Bloomer, the early suffragist and crusader for sensible clothes for women. Bloomer's home is also nearby.

"We do not expect our path will be strewn with the flowers of popular applause, but over the thorns of bigotry and prejudice will be our way, and on our banners will beat the dark storm clouds of opposition. . . . Unmoved we will bear it aloft. Undauntedly we will unfurl it to the gale . . . ," Elizabeth Cady Stanton said in her address to the convention in 1848. The words ring as heroically today as they did then. For us, they are also a reminder that even with many of the injustices of those days corrected, much still remains to be done not only for women's rights but for human rights everywhere.

A CLOSE-UP

THE FIRST WOMEN'S RIGHTS CONVENTION

On the morning of July 19, 1848 the streets of Seneca Falls were bustling as people set out for the Wesleyan Chapel. Built at the corner of Fall and Mynderse streets only five years earlier, this chapel was the place of worship for 60 people who had broken off from the Methodist Episcopal church to form the local Wesleyan Methodist Society of Seneca Falls. Wesleyan Methodist societies were being formed all over the northern states as a protest against slavery, and they took an outspoken position in favor of other reform issues such as temperance and women's rights.

Wesleyan Chapel, site of the 1848 *Women's Rights Convention* (Courtesy of the National Park Service)

From the planning stages of the new chapel the society intended to expand the structure's purpose beyond religious services. They wanted to throw open the doors of their facility for free use by reform speakers on many issues, and numerous prominent and influential figures spoke there, including abolitionist Frederick Douglass and feminist Matilda Joslyn Gage. When the Free Soil party formed in 1847–48 to oppose the extension of slavery to territories gained from Mexico, the organizers used the Wesleyan Chapel to hold their meetings. When the time came to hold the first Women's Rights Convention, the convention organizers naturally turned to this sympathetic congregation and its chapel.

On the morning of July 19, many attendees arrived early and no one had yet opened the chapel. Finally, someone gave Elizabeth Cady Stanton's nephew a boost through one of the windows so the boy could unlock the doors.

As the Convention came to order, one of the first items of business was the Declaration of Sentiments, read by Stanton. Based on the Declaration of Independence, the Declaration of Sentiments listed women's grievances against society and demanded basic rights of self-determination.

During the two-day convention, heated discussion arose over whether to include the issue of women's suffrage (the right to vote) as part of the Declaration. Finally, the document was approved, with the suffrage clause included, and 100 people signed it, 68 women and 32 men. It was the first recorded time that women's suffrage was publicly endorsed in the United States. (It's interesting to note that one-third of the signers were members of the Wesleyan Methodist Society.) Final victory came only after more than 70 years of campaigning, with ratification in 1920 of the 19th Amendment to the United States Constitution.

PRESERVING IT FOR THE FUTURE

The Women's Rights National Historic Park was authorized by Congress on December 8, 1980 and consists of 2.99 acres owned by the National Park Service and 2.74 acres of nonfederal land in Seneca Falls and nearby Waterloo, N.Y. The park includes the Wesleyan Chapel and Declaration Park, the Stanton home, the M'Clintock House, where the Declaration of Sentiments was written, a Visitor Center, and an Education and Cultural Center housing the Suffrage Press Printshop. In 1995 the park received 35,000 visitors.

The Visitor Center includes a Women's Rights Museum, where visitors can view a 25-minute award-winning film, *Dream of Equality*.

EXPLORING FURTHER

Books on Elizabeth Cady Stanton and the Women's Rights Movement

Cullen-Dupont, Kathryn. *Elizabeth Cady Stanton and Women's Liberty*. Makers of America. New York: Facts On File, 1992.

Dubois, Ellen Carol. *The Elizabeth Cady Stanton-Susan B. Anthony Reader; Correspondence, Writing, Speeches*. Boston: Northeastern University Press, 1992.

Fritz, Jean. *You Want Women to Vote, Lizzie Stanton?* New York: Putnam, 1995.

Gleiter, Jan. *Elizabeth Cady Stanton*. Austin, Tex.: Raintree/Steck-Vaughn, 1996.

Griffith, Elisabeth. *In Her Own Right: The Life of Elizabeth Cady Stanton*. New York: Oxford University Press, 1985.

McCully, Emily Arnold. *The Ballot Box Battle*. Edited by A. Levine. New York: Knopf, 1996.

Related Places

Susan B. Anthony House
17 Madison Street
Rochester, NY 14608
(716) 235-6124
Internet: http://www.frontiernet.net/~/hurst/sbahouse/index.htm

Anthony, a pioneer in women's rights, lived in this redbrick house from 1866 until her death in 1906. Here, Anthony was arrested for voting in 1872, and here too, in many of the rooms open to callers, she met with such famous visitors as Elizabeth Cady Stanton, who drafted many of Anthony's speeches, and the African-American crusader for human rights Frederick Douglass. The restored house is now a museum, filled with photographs, Anthony's memorabilia, and much of the original furniture.

Frederick Douglass National Historic Site
1411 W Street, SE
Washington, DC 20016
(202) 426-5960 or 426-5961
Internet: http://www.nps.gov/frdo/freddoug.html

Home of the great abolitionist Frederick Douglass (1818–95). Born a slave, Douglass fled to the North as a young man. He soon became one of the most eloquent speakers and writers of his time against the practice of slavery. He was also a staunch supporter of women's rights, attending the first Women's Rights Convention in Seneca Falls in 1848. On the last day of his life, February 20, 1895, Douglass attended a meeting of the National Council of Women in Washington.

Ford's Theatre National Site

SITE OF ABRAHAM LINCOLN'S ASSASSINATION
Washington, District of Columbia

AT A GLANCE

Built: Original building, 1833; current structure built 1863 after original building was destroyed by fire.

Site of Abraham Lincoln's assassination

On the night of April 14, 1865, President Abraham Lincoln was shot in Ford's Theatre by John Wilkes Booth. The president died in the early hours of April 15 in the small back bedroom of a boardinghouse across the street. The theater in which Lincoln was shot and the house where he died are preserved today as Ford's Theatre National Historic Site.

Address:
Ford's Theatre National Historic Site
511 10th Street, NW
Washington, DC 20004
(202) 426-6924
Internet: http://www.nps.gov/foth/index2.htm

It had been a long and bloody war, a time of great heartbreak and tragedy. Some call it the Civil War, some the War Between the States, but for all Americans, whether black or white, whether from the North, South, East, or West, it was the war that changed the course of American history forever. One of the great tragedies of its conclusion was the assassination of Abraham Lincoln.

At this hour the melancholy intelligence of the assassination of Mr. Lincoln, President of the United States, at Fords Theater was brought to this office, and information obtained from the following persons goes to show that the assassin is a man named J. Wilks [*sic*] Booth.

—District of Columbia Metropolitan Police Blotter,
April 14, 1865

♦♦♦♦♦

Fought between Northern states (the Union) and Southern states (the Confederacy), the U.S. Civil War began after South Carolina seceded, or withdrew, from the Union December 20, 1860, followed by six other Southern states. The fighting began on April 12, 1861 when the United States moved troops to Fort Sumter in South Carolina, and Confederate General P. G. T. Beauregard followed orders to fire on the fort. Almost immediately thereafter four more states joined the Confederacy, and the bitterest war ever experienced by Americans began.

The causes were many, and they had been festering for a long time. The war's roots lay in sectional rivalry, economic pressures, moral indignation among abolitionists about the continued practice of slavery in the South, and questions surrounding the extension of slavery to new territories as they were admitted to the Union. For the Confederates, the problem boiled down to self-determination and states' rights versus control by the federal government. In the face of Southern resistance Abraham Lincoln, newly elected president (November 1860), believed he was duty-bound to preserve the Union.

Ford's Theatre, the place where Abraham Lincoln was assassinated (Courtesy of the National Park Service)

The war lasted four ugly years, finally ending with Confederate General Robert E. Lee's surrender at Appomattox, Virginia on April 9, 1865. Ironically it was on a night of celebration, gaiety, and laughter in a brightly lit theater that one of the war's darkest tragedies occurred.

The play that night of April 14, 1865 in Ford's Theatre was an English comedy called *Our American Cousin*. It wasn't a very good play, but it was light and filled with laughter, and the people of Washington, D.C., like those elsewhere across America, were much in need of amusement after so many years of dark and bloody violence.

Violence, though, was still very much on the mind of one man in the theater that night, an actor by the name of John Wilkes Booth. Booth was a member of a famous family of actors. His father, Junius Brutus Booth, was well

Inside Ford's Theatre today (Courtesy of the National Park Service)

respected for his performances in tragedies, and his brother Edwin was a Shakespearean actor best known for his dazzling interpretation of Hamlet. John Wilkes Booth wasn't as good an actor as his illustrious relatives, but he was known for his intense passion and quick temper. He was also a Southern sympathizer and a fanatic hater of Lincoln.

Booth wasn't currently appearing in any theatrical productions, and he used his free time to plan what he hoped would be a singular blow for the Southern cause. His original plan, formed weeks before that tragic night with a gang of co-conspirators, was not to murder Lincoln but to kidnap him on March 17 and hold him in exchange for Confederate prisoners of war. That plan had fallen apart, though, when the president had changed his itinerary, and since then Southern forces had endured two disastrous defeats, leaving Lee no choice but to surrender. The war was over, but Booth still thirsted for revenge. Visiting Ford's Theatre that morning to pick up his mail, a standard practice of actors at the time, he had learned from an excited theater employee that the president would be attending that evening's performance. The State Box, reserved for special dignitaries and overlooking the stage, was being readied for the visit with the addition of a rocker, several small comfortable chairs, and a couch. A large portrait of George Washington was hung to decorate the box, and flags had been draped down the front.

There wasn't much time for careful planning, but Booth had immediately sprung into action, contacting some of his co-conspirators and informing them that he intended to assassinate the president that night. He was familiar with the play being presented and knew what lines in the comedy generally received the biggest laughs. His plan was to enter the president's box and shoot Lincoln during one of those moments of loud laughter, hoping that the noise would cover up his movements until the deed was done. His plan also required two of his fellow conspirators to participate. One of them, George Atzerodt, was to assassinate Vice President Andrew Johnson that same evening, while another, Lewis Paine (also known as Lewis Thorton Powell) was to kill Secretary of State William Seward. All three assassinations were to take place simultaneously at 10:15.

It was a daring scheme. To make certain that his part of it went through without a hitch Booth had even gone to Ford's Theatre around six o'clock that evening and invited several of the theater employees out for a drink. Returning to the theater on his own, he had examined the State Box, which

The State Box, from which Lincoln and his guests were watching the play, has been restored to its appearance at the time of his death. (Courtesy of the National Park Service)

could be entered by passing through two separate doors parted by a small vestibule. He had then used a small tool to drill a tiny hole in the inside door, allowing him to peer in and ascertain the positions of the people inside.

It was a war-weary Lincoln who entered Ford's Theatre that night. The last few years had been long and difficult, and he had aged perceptibly. With the president were his wife, Mary Todd Lincoln; Major H. R. Rathbone; and the major's fiancée, Clara Harris. All were escorted to the State Box. Later reports by witnesses were contradictory as to whether a guard was posted at the outside door of the box or not. The president frequently traveled about Washington without one. If there was a guard (none ever came forth after the assassination to so testify), he was either not in position at the time or had been deceived in some way into allowing Lincoln's assassin to enter.

What *is* certain is that shortly after 10:00 P.M. John Wilkes Booth entered the lobby of Ford's Theatre, climbed the stairway to the Dress Circle, and made his way through the outer door of the State Box.

On stage the play was in progress and nearly 1,700 people seated throughout the theater were enjoying the antics of the actress Laura Keene and her fellow performers. Soon an actor named Harry Hawk would be on stage to deliver one of the play's funniest lines. That was the moment Booth was waiting for.

As the laughter in the theater began to swell he quietly opened the inner door. There in the darkness the president was sitting with the other members of his party, watching the stage. The rest happened quickly.

Aiming a small, .44-caliber single-shot derringer at a spot behind Lincoln's left ear, Booth pulled the trigger.

The shot sent the president reeling forward as Mrs. Lincoln tried to hold him in her arms. Whether Booth had originally planned to escape the same way he entered or not is unclear, but suddenly he was attacked by Major Rathbone, who grappled with him. Drawing a dagger, Booth stabbed the major in the left arm and attempted to escape by leaping onto the stage. He had done such acrobatics many times in the past during some of his dramatic performances, but this time his foot caught on something, either a piece of drapery or one of the newly hung flags. Thrown off balance he landed awkwardly 12 feet below on the stage floor, breaking a small bone in his left leg.

Either before or after leaping—there is contradictory evidence on this point—Booth shouted, "Sic semper tyrannis," a Latin phrase which was also on the Virginia State flag, meaning "Thus always unto tyrants!" Then, limping on his injured leg, he hurried across the stage and out the back stage door where he had a horse waiting to help him make his escape.

The theater erupted into panic. In the State Box Major Rathbone managed to get to the door and summon help before collapsing from the effects of his wound. Among the first to enter was a young doctor, 23-year-old Charles Leale. Leale made a quick examination of the president, who had been stretched out on the floor of the box, and discovered the bullet hole in the back of his head.

As Booth met up with a fellow conspirator David Herold, Dr. Leale and a group of military men were carrying the unconscious president down the stairs of the theater and out into the street. The mob gathering outside the theater was quickly becoming uncontrollable, and under the circumstances, the White House was too far away. Needing to get the stricken Lincoln to a safe bed, Leale and the military men heard a man calling to them from a boardinghouse across the street to bring the president inside.

There, in Petersen's Boarding House, on April 15, 1865, at 7:22 A.M., Abraham Lincoln died.

Eleven days later, on April 26, 1865, John Wilkes Booth was shot and killed inside a burning tobacco shed by army soldiers who had pursued him to a small farm near Bowling Green, Virginia. David Herold, who was in the shed with Booth, surrendered peacefully.

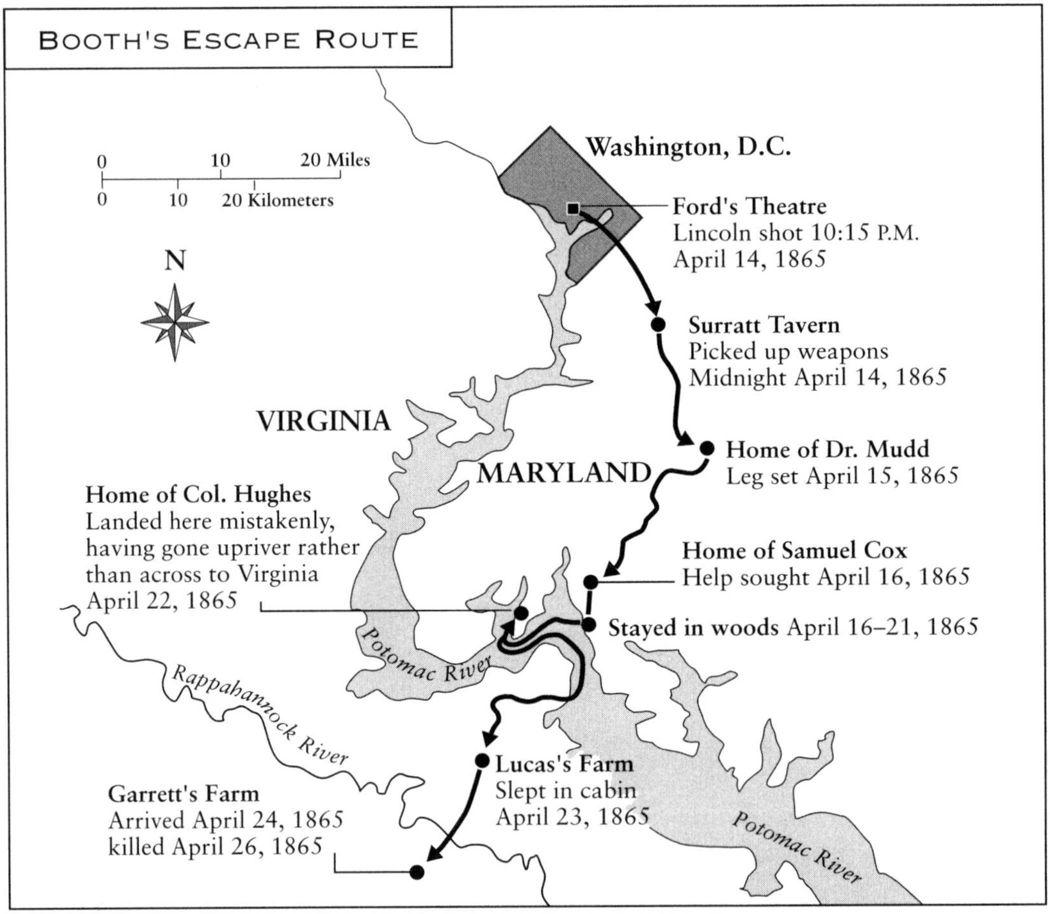

The escape route taken by John Wilkes Booth the night of April 14, 1865

Following his orders, Lewis Paine had entered Secretary of State Seward's house on the night of April 14. Paine pistol-whipped Seward's son and attacked the secretary of state with a knife, seriously wounding him. The wounds, however, were not fatal, and Paine was captured three days after the attack. For reasons unknown, George Atzerodt never attempted to carry out the assassination of Vice President Andrew Johnson.

Tried before a military commission, Paine, Atzerodt, Herold, and Mary Surratt, in whose boardinghouse the conspirators had met to work out their plans, were found guilty and hanged. Four others also implicated in the assassination plan were sentenced to prison terms. Controversy still exists as to the degrees of guilt of these individuals, particularly in the cases of Mary Surratt and Dr. Samuel Mudd, who treated Booth's broken leg during his frantic escape attempt.

Today, restored to its original condition at the time of Lincoln's assassination, Ford's Theatre is still a working theater producing musicals and plays that "embody family values, underscore multiculturalism, and illuminate the eclectic character of American life." A National Historic Site operated by the National Park Service, the theater offers talks and tours by park rangers who are steeped in the history of the place and its significance. Visitors can view the State Box where Lincoln sat as he watched the play that fateful night. As one historian remarked as he stood on the Ford's Theatre stage, you won't find Mr. Lincoln at the Lincoln Memorial—"If you want to find Mr. Lincoln, you have to look here." One feels the presence of this great man, whose love of theater and music illustrates the roundness and humanity of his character. The box has been furnished to appear much as it did then, based on photographs taken just a few days after the event, down to the portrait of Washington hung on the wall in Lincoln's honor.

You can also stand on the stage where Booth jumped following the shooting. In the theater's basement, you can visit a museum where mementos and historical objects are on display. The Petersen boardinghouse across the street, also a National Historic Site, is also open to the public, restored to look much as it did the night President Lincoln died there.

The visit is an extraordinary experience, both sobering and intellectually stimulating. It is the place where a truly great American met his end. In the words of lecturer and orator Robert G. Ingersoll, "Lincoln was not a type.

He stands alone—no ancestors, no fellows, no successors." Those words were spoken in 1894, and they still ring true today.

A CLOSE-UP: PETERSEN'S BOARDING HOUSE

Petersen's Boarding House was an unpretentious three-story building located across the street from the theater. Most of the boarders were out the night of April 14–15, 1865, but one, Henry Safford, had by chance decided to stay home.

As the entourage carrying the mortally wounded president proceeded slowly down the staircase in Ford's Theatre and then exited to 10th Street, Dr. Charles Leale, who was attending Lincoln, realized he had to find someplace nearby where he could minister to his illustrious patient. He described the events that followed in a letter written two years later, in July 1867:

> The crowd in the street completely obstructed the doorway and a captain, whose services proved invaluable all through the night, came to me, saying: "Surgeon, give me your commands and I will see that they are obeyed." I asked him to clear a passage to the nearest house opposite. He had on side arms and drew his sword. With the sword and word of command he cleared the way. We slowly crossed the street. It was necessary to stop several times to give me the opportunity to remove the clot of blood from the opening to the wound. A barrier of men had been formed to keep back the crowds on each side of an open space leading to the house. Those who went ahead reported that the house directly opposite the theatre was closed. I saw a man standing at the door of Mr. Petersen's house, diagonally opposite, holding a lighted candle in his hand and beckoning us to enter.

The boarder, Henry Safford, also described the events in a letter written in 1903:

> I had spent the evening reading in the front room when, about ten o'clock, hearing a disturbance outside, I went to the window and learned that Lincoln had been shot. I hastened down to the front door, and, while standing on the upper steps, the President was brought out of the theatre and into the street towards where I stood. Suddenly those carrying him seemed in doubt as to where they would take him. Quickly realizing the cause of their hesitation, although being alone in the house, I took the responsibility of crying out, "Bring him in here, Bring him in here," which invitation was immediately accepted and he was taken to the bedroom in the rear of the parlors and placed on a bed.

Today Petersen's Boarding House evokes the lifestyle of a mid-19th-century boardinghouse, a modest environment in which the man who was born in a log cabin would have felt comfortable. But on that long night, he was not aware of his surroundings. Today, the simple room with its bedstead too small for the president's six-foot-four-inch frame serves as a somber reminder of those tragic last hours of life and the desperate attempts made by his physicians to save him.

PRESERVING IT FOR THE FUTURE

Originally built as a Baptist church in 1833, the building now called Ford's Theatre has had an eventful past. It was leased in 1861 by John T. Ford for use as a theater, which was successful. After renovations in 1862, Ford reopened it as Ford's Athenaeum, but the building burned, and Ford rebuilt the theater, this time opening in 1863 with the name Ford's New Theatre.

The theater was closed in 1865 after Lincoln's assassination, and the War Department leased the building from Ford later that year, converting it into an office building. In 1866, the United States Congress purchased the building for $100,000. The government used it variously as a medical library and museum and War Department office building until the three-story structure suffered an interior collapse in 1893, resulting in the death of 22 government clerks and the injury of 68.

After use for eight years as a warehouse, the building was transferred from the War Department to the Office of Public Buildings and Public Parks in 1928. At that time a saloon that had been added was torn down, and the Lincoln Museum opened on the first floor of the old Ford's Theatre building in 1932. That same year the building was transferred to the jurisdiction of the National Park Service.

Restoration of Ford's Theatre was first proposed to Congress in 1946 and was finally approved in 1964. Renovation took three years, and the theater reopened on February 13, 1968. On June 23, 1970, Congress established Ford's Theatre National Historic Site, made up of Ford's Theatre and Petersen's Boarding House—with Ford's Theatre now used both as an active theater and a historic site.

EXPLORING FURTHER

Books about Ford's Theatre and Abraham Lincoln

Good, Timothy S. *We Saw Lincoln Shot: One Hundred Eyewitness Accounts.* Oxford, Miss.: University Press of Mississippi, 1995.

Hanchett, William. *The Lincoln Murder Conspiracies.* Urbana and Chicago, Ill.: University of Illinois Press, 1983.

Kent, Zachary. *The Story of Ford's Theatre and the Death of Lincoln.* Chicago: Children's Press, 1987.

Kunhardt, Dorothy Monserve. *Twenty Days: A Narrative in Text and Pictures of the Assassination of Abraham Lincoln.* New York: Harper and Row, 1965. Reprint. N. Hollywood: Newcastle Publishing, 1985.

Lewis, Lloyd, and Mark E. Neely, Jr. *The Assassination of Lincoln: History and Myth.* Lincoln, Neb.: University of Nebraska Press, 1994.

McHale, John E., Jr. *Dr. Samuel A. Mudd and the Lincoln Assassination.* People in Focus. Parsippany, N.J.: Dillon Press, 1994.

O'Neal, Michael. *The Assassination of Abraham Lincoln: Opposing Viewpoints.* Great Mysteries. San Diego: Greenhaven Press, 1991.

Reck, William Emerson. *A. Lincoln: His Last 24 Hours.* Jefferson, N.C.: McFarland and Company, Inc., 1987.

Surratt House Museum
9118 Brandywine Road
P.O. Box 427
Clinton, MD 20735
Telephone: (301) 868-1121
Fax: (301) 868-8177
Internet: http://www.glue.umd.edu/~clwspoon/surratt.html

When John Wilkes Booth ran out of Ford's Theatre after shooting President Lincoln on April 14, 1865, he fled from Washington, D.C. to the nearby Maryland countryside. There, he picked up weapons from alleged co-conspirator Mary Surratt, who was later found guilty of conspiracy to assassinate the president, although evidence is now inconclusive that she knew about the plan to kill Lincoln. Executed in 1865, she was the first woman to be put to death by the federal government. Today, her residence—which, among other uses, also served as a tavern and as a Confederate underground rendezvous during the Civil War—has become a museum, dedicated in part to telling her side of the story.

The Surratt Museum, located in the Surratt House, contains eight rooms furnished in the original 1850–1865 style. Guides in period costume lead tours, and the museum presents a variety of programs and events recapturing the history of mid-19th-century life while focusing on the story of the Lincoln conspiracy. Next door to Surratt House, a Visitor's Center features permanent exhibits on the Surratt family and the Lincoln assassination, as well as a library containing over 1,200 books dealing with the Civil War and the assassination.

One of the most popular and interesting events sponsored by the Surratt Society, which operates the house, is its John Wilkes Booth escape route tour held each year. The tour covers Booth's route from Ford's Theatre in Washington, D.C. to the farm on which he was killed in Bowling Green, Virginia.

Dr. Samuel A. Mudd Home (1830)
Route 232
Waldorf, MD 20646

(301) 934-8464
http://www.somd.lib.md.us/MUSEUMS/mudd.htm

The physician's home where John Wilkes Booth went to have his broken leg set after he fatally shot President Lincoln in 1865, the house is still owned by members of the Mudd family. The Mudd house is now a museum, featuring original furniture from Dr. Mudd's time, including the red plush couch where Booth sat as he sought treatment for his injury. You can also see the bedroom in which Booth slept after Dr. Mudd treated his leg. Guides offer talks about the Lincoln assassination, stressing Mudd's part of the story. Mudd was a Southern sympathizer who had met several times with Booth before the assassination, but he claimed not to have been involved in the assassination plot. Nevertheless, Mudd was sentenced to prison for his involvement with Booth, and his descendants are still actively engaged in trying to establish his innocence. Dr. Mudd was officially pardoned in 1869 by President Andrew Johnson for his heroic activities during a yellow-fever epidemic that broke out at Fort Jefferson, the prison in the Florida Keys where he had been incarcerated.

Lincoln Home National Historic Site
413 South Eighth Street
Springfield, IL 62701-1905
(217) 492-4150

This two-story home of Abraham Lincoln was constructed in 1839. The Lincolns lived in this house from 1844 until Lincoln's inauguration in 1861. Restored to its appearance of the 1860s, the home stands in the middle of a four-block historic district that the National Park Service is also restoring to capture the flavor of the neighborhood as it was in Lincoln's time.

The Jane Addams Hull-House Museum

HOME AND FIRST COMMUNITY CENTER OF
SOCIAL REFORMER JANE ADDAMS
Chicago, Illinois

AT A GLANCE

Built: 1856

Opened in 1889 by Jane Addams as a settlement house called Hull-House.

In this Italianate structure, one of the oldest residential buildings in Chicago, Addams and her associates lived and worked, providing a wide variety of social services to Chicago's poor.

Address:
Jane Addams Hull-House Museum
800 South Halsted Street
University of Illinois at Chicago
Chicago, IL 60617-7017
(312) 413-5353
Internet: http://www.uic.edu/jaddams/hull/hull-house.html

In 1889, Jane Addams opened a community center in a neglected old mansion at 800 South Halsted Street in Chicago. Aided by Ellen Gates Starr, Addams helped hundreds of Chicago immigrants and others gain a place of self-respect in society. Her campaigns for social and labor reforms became world renowned, and she won a Nobel Peace Prize in 1931.

Deeds make habits, habits make character,
character makes destiny!

—Jane Addams, from her college journal ca. 1881

♦♦♦♦♦

As the old adage says, "Charity begins at home." For the settlement house workers of the late 1800s, "home" was wherever charity was needed. The movement started in England in 1884 when an Anglican clergyman, Samuel A. Barnett, founded Toynbee Hall in the slums of London. Barnett's idea was to have volunteers (in the case of Toynbee Hall, primarily university men) "settle" or take up residence in buildings located in underprivileged areas. There the volunteers would reside and be part of the daily life in the area they were serving. The building, or settlement house, then would also become the hub of the residents' charitable activities, drawing those in need to it. This way, Barnett believed, his volunteers would not

Jane Addams' Hull-House became a center to serve the surrounding community in Chicago. Today it is a museum commemorating her life and work. (Courtesy of Jane Addams Hull-House Museum)

only help to relieve the poverty and despair of the slums but, being generally from the privileged class, would also learn something about the way the real world operated.

Barnett's idea found adherents in the late 1800s, when people were beginning to understand the consequences of the Industrial Revolution, which had swept through Europe and North America between 1750 and 1850. Many great positive and dramatic changes occurred in the social and economic structure of the world as new technologies and inventions created the factory system and mass production. But the Industrial Revolution also had drawbacks. Too often, careless operation of factories and mines produced environmental blight, and an ever-increasing number of people were forced to shift from an agricultural economy to an industrial one. The laboring population, formerly scattered through small towns and farmlands, suddenly found itself relocated in cities and large urban areas. Here, dangerously overcrowded living conditions, poor housing, poor wages, and backbreaking work took a heavy toll on mind, body, and spirit.

The settlement house movement came to America in 1886 when Stanton Coit founded Neighborhood House on the Lower East Side of New York City. The most famous of all the settlement houses was begun three years later, in 1889, when Jane Addams and her former college classmate Ellen Gates Starr joined together with a group of women associates to found Hull-House on the Near West Side of Chicago, in a neighborhood made up mostly of Italians, Russian and Polish Jews, Irish, Germans, Greeks, and Bohemians.

As Addams later explained,

> . . . I gradually became convinced, that it would be a good thing to rent a house in a part of the city where many primitive and actual needs are found in which young women who have been given over too exclusively to study, might restore a balance of activity along traditional lines and learn of life from life itself, where they might try out some of the things they had been taught. . . .

The Industrial Revolution came late to America, not developing in full force until the years immediately following the Civil War. But, when it came, it came with a fury, drawing not just Americans but hundreds of thousands of hopeful immigrants to the nation's big cities. They came with the dream of finding good jobs and starting new lives. Instead many found poverty, hardship, and despair. For the immigrants particularly, life in the big cities was difficult. Far from their native homes, most speaking a halting and hesitant English, and some not even that, and possessing very little money upon arrival, they swelled the already overpopulated city ghettos. By 1890 a full 80 percent of the people living in Chicago were immigrants or the children of immigrants. With few cities willing or able to muster the resources to accommodate such a massive influx, poverty and disease inside the city ghettos swelled to epidemic proportions.

Jane Addams ca. 1889, *about the time she founded* Hull-House (Courtesy of Jane Addams Hull-House Museum, University of Illinois at Chicago)

Writing in 1907, Jane Addams described the conditions inside America's cities: "It has been well said that the modern city is a stronghold of industrialism, quite as the feudal city was a stronghold of militarism, but the modern city fears no enemies, and rivals from without and its problems of government are solely internal. Affairs for the most part are going badly in these great new centres in which the quickly congregated population has not yet learned to arrange its affairs satisfactorily, insanitary housing, poisonous sewage, contaminated water, infant mortality, the spread of contagion, adulterated food, impure milk, smoke-laden air, ill-ventilated factories, dangerous occupations, juvenile crime, unwholesome crowding . . . are the enemies which the modern city must face and overcome. . . ."

The charter of Hull-House, as written by Addams, defined its intended mission: "To provide a center for higher civic and social life: to institute and maintain educational and philanthropic enterprises, and to investigate and improve the conditions in the industrial districts of Chicago." It was a mission that Addams and her associates more than fulfilled.

Addams, born in Cedarville, Illinois in 1860, came from a privileged family. Her father, John Huy Addams, was a successful businessman and politician who had been raised as a Quaker. When Jane was only two years old, her mother died; her father raised her almost on his own, and she grew to adore him. As a young woman, Jane attended Rockford College, graduating in 1881. She went on to the Women's Medical College in Philadelphia, Pennsylvania, but a serious back ailment forced her to drop out after her first year. After undergoing an operation and spending six months in bed, she traveled to Europe. On one of her visits to London she saw the Toynbee Hall Settlement House in action and began to think of organizing a similar project in America. The death of her father in 1881 made her economically self-sufficient, but like many other intelligent and energetic women of her time, she long sought to find a place for herself in a society that thought of women only as wives, mothers, and homemakers. Samuel Barnett's settlement house concept, with its intention of not only aiding those in need but also giving the more fortunate a chance to benefit society, immediately struck her as being both sound and valuable.

The building Addams and her associates chose for their settlement house in 1889 was a run-down mansion in the overcrowded slums of Chicago's Near West Side. Originally built in 1856 as a country home by wealthy realtor Charles Hull, it had long since fallen into disrepair among the tenements and sweatshops that surrounded it. The neighborhood residents had taken to calling the place "the old Hull House," and so Hull-House was adopted as the official name of the settlement.

When it first opened, Hull-House provided services that included reading classes, warm meals, a kindergarten and day care center, an employment bureau, and classes in music, art, and literature. (The great jazz musician Benny Goodman later learned to play clarinet in Hull-House.) In the years following 1889, about a dozen other buildings were added to house classes and clubs, a nursery school, the only library in the neighborhood, and one of the first gymnasiums in the country. Many of the local residents, lacking bathrooms, came to the center for weekly baths. By the early 1900s the activities in Hull-House, which took up a full city block, had branched out to include a cooperative residence for working women called the Jane Club, a theater, a meeting hall for trade union groups, playgrounds and gymnasiums, and myriad clubs and programs for educational, vocational, and domestic training.

As the Hull-House settlement grew, its influence extended far beyond the immediate neighborhood and into the wider social and political arena. Working with other reformers, Addams and her associates founded the Immigrants Protective League to safeguard the rights of newly arrived immigrants, the Juvenile Protective League, the first juvenile court in America, and the first Juvenile Psychopathic Clinic. They pushed for and won strong protective legislation for women and children in Illinois, and in 1903 they secured the passage of the state's first major child labor law and an accompanying compulsory education law. The creation of the Federal Children's Bureau on a national level in 1912 and the passage of federal child labor laws in 1916 resulted in large part from the influence of Addams and the example of activities at Hull-House.

Today, only the original mansion and an adjoining dining hall are left standing on the site of what was once the Hull-House settlement. The shifting focus of the nation during World War I, changing patterns in immigration, financial difficulties, and the gradually increasing professionalism of social work—with less emphasis on social changes and more on psychiatric adjustment—dimmed the luster of Addams's settlement house movement, and it no longer stood in the vanguard of national reform. In its time, though, the settlement house movement was a major force in urban American life and an indispensable vehicle for social reform. In 1897 there were 74 different settlement houses operating in the United States. In 1900, the number topped 100, and by 1910 more than 400 spread throughout the nation not only in big cities like Chicago, New York, and Boston but in many smaller cities and towns as well. While few traditional settlement houses operate today, the spirit of the movement survives in thousands of social service centers throughout the nation. They go by other names, such as "neighborhood centers," but they still stand in the front lines in the ongoing battle against poverty and despair in America's cities.

Throughout her years at Hull-House, Jane Addams became one of America's most famous citizens. Through her work at the settlement and outside, and through her 11 books and hundreds of articles, she fought continually for human rights and reform. In 1910, she became the first woman to receive an honorary degree from Yale University, and in 1912, she was the first woman to second the nomination of a presidential candidate (Theodore Roosevelt) at a national political convention. Once called "the most dangerous woman in America" by the Daughters of the American Revolution for her pacifism during World War I, in 1931 she became the first American woman to win the Nobel Peace Prize. Among many of her other accomplishments, she served as president of the Women's International League for Peace and Freedom from 1919 until her death, and in the 1920s she helped to found the American Civil Liberties Union (ACLU).

Jane Addams died in Chicago on May 21, 1935. She was buried in Cedarville, her childhood home.

Today, Hull-House lives on in the form of the Hull-House Association. Operating through 6 community centers and 35 other locations throughout Chicago, the association serves 225,000 children, families, and individuals each year. It operates nearly a hundred programs encouraging self-reliance and focusing on foster care, child care, job training, counseling, home delivered meals, advocacy, programs in literacy, and much more. Still pursuing Addams's original goal of "neighbors helping neighbors," the Hull-House Association continues the fight the great reformer began—the fight to bring a brighter future to the children of our cities.

A CLOSE-UP: LIFE AT HULL-HOUSE

In 1929, the start of the Great Depression, when work was scarce and for many people food was even scarcer, a young man named James Velde knocked on the door of Hull-House on Chicago's West Side. Although he had recently graduated from Harvard Law School, because of the nation's faltering economy he, like many others, couldn't find a job. He knew a little about the 13-building complex—his college roommate's sisters were social workers and had spent a summer there. Velde pursued his roommate's recommenda-

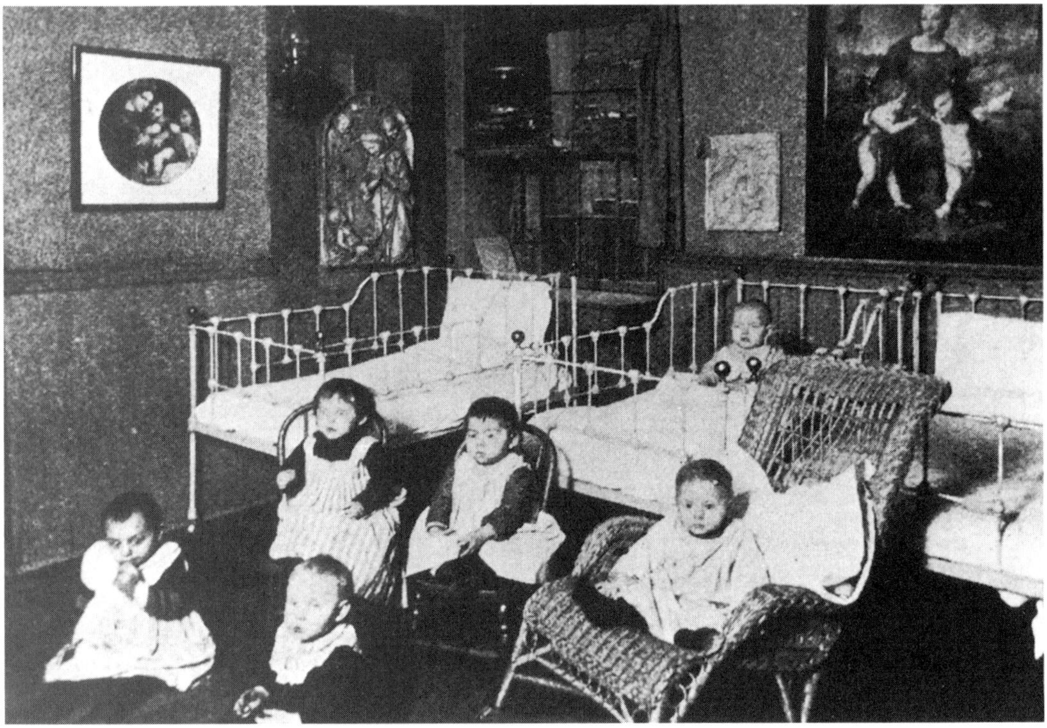

A kindergarten at Hull-House in the 1890s (Courtesy of Jane Addams Hull-House Museum, University of Illinois at Chicago)

tion to house there; his roommate characterized Hull-House as "an interesting place to be," Velde later recalled.

By this time, Jane Addams had been running Hull-House for 30 years. Velde paid $15 a month for a tiny one-room apartment at Hull-House, with a view of Halsted Street. Streetcars rumbled by under his window day and night. Thirty other residents, male and female, lived there, too, and the constant hustle and bustle kept things hopping. On the floors below Velde's room activities were constant—sewing classes, kindergarten classes, comings and goings in art galleries, literary clubs, and all the dozens of other activities that made this house the center of the neighborhood.

And it was still the home of Jane Addams. Always referred to as "Miss Addams," "She would preside over the house," Velde recalled when he was 91. "She was a very pleasant and friendly person. She wasn't overpowering, rather very low key. But Miss Addams asked penetrating questions."

Residents all put in time "on the door," as they called it, sitting at the front reception area to answer phones and questions and making sure that the house remained safe from the bloody skirmishes that sometimes took place in the neighborhood.

"Beyond any question," Velde said, "the relationships with people was the best part about living at Hull-House. It was almost like a collegiate atmosphere." Dinners were relaxing and cordial, with residents, guests, and Addams conversing informally after the meal. "You could be sitting next to anyone," Velde said, and he met several famous people during the five years he lived at Hull-House. He also met his wife, Esther, whom he married in 1934.

In 1930 Jane Addams gave Velde a brief handwritten note of recommendation for a volunteer position with the Legal Aid Bureau. The note was magic, opening doors even his Harvard degree hadn't budged. He began work at the bureau, providing legal advice and teaching English to immigrants. That experience landed him a job with a small law firm a year later. It was the beginning of a long, successful career—one of many that Jane Addams helped to launch.

PRESERVING IT FOR THE FUTURE

In the early 1960s most of the buildings of the two-block Hull-House complex were leveled (amid worldwide protest) by the University of Illinois to make way for the construction of a Chicago campus. The original Hull mansion was restored by the university, however, in the mid-1960s, with much of the furniture used by Jane Addams remaining intact. The interior of this building, where Addams and Ellen Gates Starr began their world-famous social settlement, has been restored to look as it did in their early days at Hull-House. Inside, original furnishings, paintings, memorabilia, photographs, and rotating exhibits re-create the history of the settlement and the work of Addams, Starr, and the other residents.

Next door is the Residents' Dining Hall, added to Hull-House in 1905. On the first floor visitors find an extensive exhibit on the history of the surrounding neighborhood as it appeared around the turn of the century. Laid out to correspond to the geography of the area, this exhibit forms part of an ongoing project to present and interpret the history of this important urban community.

An introductory slide program is available to drop-in visitors in conjunction with the tours. Special programs on topics relating to the history of Hull-House and the neighborhood are also available to groups making reservations in advance.

Hull-House became a National Historic Landmark in 1967 and a Chicago Landmark in 1974. In the words of Dr. Murray H. Nelligan of the National Park Service, "In my opinion, none of the national historical landmarks better signifies the achievements of the past while pointing the way to a brighter future for our cities than does Hull House."

EXPLORING FURTHER

Books about Jane Addams

Davis, Allen F. *American Heroine: The Life and Legend of Jane Addams.* London: Oxford University Press, 1973.

Deegan, Mary Jo. *Jane Addams and the Men of the Chicago School, 1892–1918.* New Brunswick, N.J.: Transaction Books, 1988.

Farrell, John C. *Beloved Lady: A History of Jane Addams Ideas on Reform and Peace.* Baltimore, Md.: Johns Hopkins University Press, 1967.

Gilbert, Miriam. *Jane Addams: World Neighbor.* Makers of America. New York: Abingdon Press, 1960.

Gleiter, Jan, and Kathleen Thompson. *Jane Addams.* Milwaukee, Wis.: Raintree Steck-Vaughn, 1987.

Kittredge, Mary. *Jane Addams.* American Women of Achievement Series. New York: Chelsea House Publishers, 1988.

Levine, Daniel. *Jane Addams and the Liberal Tradition.* Madison, Wis.: State Historical Society of Wisconsin, 1971.

Meigs, Cornelia. *Jane Addams: Pioneer for Social Justice.* Boston: Little, Brown and Company, 1970.

Mooney, Elizabeth Comstock. *Jane Addams*. Library of American Heroes. Chicago: Follett Publishing Co., 1968.
Polacheck, Hilda Satt. *I Came a Stranger: The Story of a Hull-House Girl*. Urbana, Ill.: University of Illinois, 1989.

Books by Jane Addams

Addams, Jane. *Twenty Years at Hull-House*. New York: Macmillan, 1910. Reprint, with an introduction and notes by James Hurt. Urbana: University of Illinois Press, 1990.
———. *Democracy and Social Ethics*. New York: Macmillan, 1902. Reprint. Cambridge: Harvard University Press-Belknap Press, 1964.
Bryan, Mary Lynn McCree, and Allen F. Davis, eds. *100 Years at Hull-House*. Bloomington, Ind.: Indiana University Press, 1990.
Johnson, Emily Cooper, ed. *Jane Addams: A Centennial Reader*. New York: Macmillan, 1960.
Lasch, Joseph, ed. *The Social Thought of Jane Addams*. American Heritage Series. Indianapolis: Bobbs-Merrill Co., 1965.

Related Place

Ida B. Wells-Barnett House
3624 S. Martin Luther King Jr. Dr.
Chicago, IL 60653
(private)

Viewable from the street, although not open to the public, this private house was the home of social reformer and crusading newspaper reporter Ida B. Wells from 1919 to 1928. Wells (1862–1931) was born a slave in Mississippi. Orphaned as an adolescent, she also lost three siblings to yellow fever. After attending Rust University and Fisk University, she became a teacher, activist, and writer who led a national campaign against lynching. As a result, her Memphis, Tennessee newspaper office was attacked by a mob and destroyed in 1892. A crusader for African-American rights and women's suffrage, she was an ally of W. E. B. DuBois, and like DuBois, she advocated a more aggressive approach to civil rights than that adopted by the National Association for the Advancement of Colored People (NAACP).

Clara Barton House

HOME AND OFFICES OF AMERICAN RED CROSS FOUNDER
CLARA BARTON
Glen Echo, Maryland

AT A GLANCE

Built: ca. 1891

38-room wood-frame house; Red Cross warehouse 1891–97; Red Cross headquarters, 1897–1904; home of Clara Barton, 1897–1912

Barton, the major figure in the founding of the American Red Cross, spent the last 15 years of her life in this house.

Address:
Clara Barton National Historic Site
5801 Oxford Road
Glen Echo, MD 20812
(301) 492-6245
Internet: http://www.nps.gov/clba

Strongwilled and driven by a humanitarian conscience, Clara Barton worked hard and long to bring relief to those suffering the tragedy of war and natural disasters. The establishment of the American Red Cross remains her shining gift to her country.

The paths of charity are over the roadways of ashes, and he who would tread them must be prepared to meet opposition, misconstruction, jealousy and calumny. Let his work be that of angels, still it will not satisfy all.

—Clara Barton

♦♦♦♦♦

When Clara Barton had a large new house built in the small town of Glen Echo, Maryland in 1891, she incorporated into it planks from houses destroyed in the Great Johnstown Flood of 1889. Somehow that act symbolizes much about the complex personality of the woman known during her time as the "angel of the battlefield."

"It will not be an elegant house, as some, but it will serve the purposes that we believe are necessary," Barton wrote at the time. Her plan was to use the large rambling house not only as a home but also as a warehouse for disaster relief supplies for the American Red Cross, which she had founded in 1881 at the age of 59. By 1897 the house, following further modifications, had become the organization's headquarters as well as a living residence for Barton and her supporting staff of volunteers.

For Clara Barton, her life and the life of the American Red Cross were one, with no separation between the two. In that viewpoint lay her strength and her greatness, as well as her weakness and her tragedy.

Born on December 25, 1821 in Oxford, Massachusetts, Clara was the youngest of five children. Her father owned a prosperous sawmill, but her mother apparently suffered from some kind of mental instability. The trait had been passed on to Clara's eldest sister who, in those days when little was understood about mental illness, was so difficult to control that she was kept

Clara Barton, photo by Matthew Brady (Courtesy of the American Red Cross)

in a locked room; on one occasion she escaped and attacked a relative with an ax.

It wasn't an easy childhood, and although close to her busy father, Clara was left pretty much on her own most of the time. Small and active—she stood barely five feet tall when fully grown—Barton found her calling at an early age when she spent two years nursing her brother David through a long and difficult illness. Part of her nursing duties including applying leeches to David's body daily. It was a fairly standard remedy for many illnesses at the time and 11-year-old Clara hardly blinked at performing the unpleasant duty. The work provided something that had been missing in her childhood—a sense of self-worth, power, and amid the chaotic lifestyle of her family, a way of gaining attention.

By the age of 15 Barton was working as a teacher, and by the time she had reached young womanhood she had organized the first free school in Bordentown, New Jersey. But eventually the townspeople decided the school was becoming too big for a woman and replaced Barton with a male teacher. Barton resigned in anger and disgust. Not long afterward she suffered the first of a series of nervous breakdowns, which troubled her throughout her life.

After recovering from her breakdown Barton entered government service as a clerk in the Patent Office in Washington, D.C. She was one of the few women in the United States to hold a government position at the time.

The Civil War, however, was the force that changed the direction of Clara Barton's life forever and began to establish her legend. There were many other civilians—including such now-famous figures as the poet Walt Whitman and the writer Louisa May Alcott—who volunteered to aid the wounded during the horrible years of America's great internal conflict. But in any accounting, Clara Barton's name must stand among the highest on the list.

At first she volunteered to help organize shipments of medicine and supplies to the hospitals and front lines, but soon she was much more intimately involved. Some stories say that Barton's father convinced her from his deathbed that she could more effectively aid the wounded by moving into the front lines and helping to nurse them. But all anyone knows for certain is that she did make this decision. Her place, she decided, was "anywhere between the bullet and the hospital." By nature somewhat timid and shy, she did not find it an easy decision to make.

At times Barton worked with such civilian relief agencies as the U.S. Christian Commission and the U.S. Sanitary Commission, but most of the time she preferred to work alone. She liked to be directly in charge, with no superiors to report to and no unwieldy organizational structure to stand in her way. And she did get things done. During those violent and bloody years she personally aided thousands of sick, wounded, and dying soldiers, finding herself at times in the thick of battles as far south as Charleston, Virginia. Wherever there were soldiers in need of aid, there was Clara Barton—at the battlefields of Cedar Mountain, Second Bull Run, Chantilly, South Mountain, Antietam. In June 1864 she was officially appointed a superintendent of nurses.

The stories of her courage and heroism became legendary. Sometimes she told these stories herself, occasionally exaggerating, but usually there was little need for exaggeration. Her deeds spoke quite eloquently of her courage.

"Men have worshipped war till it has cost a million times more than the whole earth is worth," Barton wrote. "Deck it as you will, war is Hell. . . . Only the desire to soften some of its hardships and allay some of its miseries ever induced me . . . to face its pestilent and unholy breath."

After the war Barton was still trying to "soften some of its hardships" by organizing an office for locating soldiers who were listed as missing by the War Department. She fought to have the prison yard inside the notorious Andersonville prison turned into a national cemetery. As she became famous, she also began to speak out for other causes, promoting voting rights for former slaves and becoming a staunch supporter of the growing feminist movement. People began to write about her. Sometimes, anonymously, she wrote about herself. Always she worked long and hard. After embarking on a long and difficult lecture tour, she suffered another nervous breakdown in 1869.

Sent to Europe to recover, Barton set to work again. The Franco-Prussian War had broken out, and she offered to help tend wounded soldiers. But her assistance was refused because she was a woman, and so she set out to organize her own relief effort, this time aiding the suffering civilians of war-torn France and Germany. During this period she learned of the existence of the International Red Cross. The organization had been founded in 1863 at the urging of Jean-Henri Dunant, a Swiss citizen who had seen the suffering and terrors of war firsthand. In 1864 the Geneva Convention adopted the

The central salon in Clara Barton's house was lined with wood panels, behind which storage rooms held bandages, clothing, and other disaster relief supplies. (Courtesy of the American Red Cross)

Red Cross as a symbol of neutral aid. The convention, attended by representatives of 26 nations, had ended with each nation's pledge to observe humanitarian rules of war regarding prisoners, wounded and sick soldiers, and civilians in war zones.

The International Red Cross was a mission that Clara Barton could believe in. In 1873 she returned to America, determined to establish her own organization along similar lines. Plagued by her continuing ill health and the indifference of public officials, she faced a long and difficult fight. But in 1881, she became president of the American Red Cross. In 1882 the United States Senate finally ratified the Geneva Convention, and by doing so officially established the Red Cross in the United States.

As president from 1881 to 1904, Barton ran the Red Cross with amazing efficiency and splendid effectiveness. While reporting on the effects of a hurricane on the Sea Islands off Georgia's coast in 1883, the writer Joel Chandler Harris had a chance to witness Barton's organization up close. The

Red Cross, he noted, was "entirely different from any other relief organization that has come under my observation. Its strongest and most admirable feature is its extreme simplicity." The "simplicity" came at a price, though. For both good and bad, under Barton's leadership it was a one-woman show, an operation that she dictated with an iron hand. "I must attend to all business myself," she wrote, and despite her poor health and the increasing protests of associates, she made all of the organization's decisions and personally managed all of its funds. She made no apologies, gave no explanations, and made little effort to compromise with others inside or outside of the organization. The International American Red Cross, as it became officially known in 1893, was, in her mind, *her* organization. She had fought for it, established it, lived it. Under her guidance, the organization's duties and activities had been expanded beyond the battlefields of war to meet the needs of those suffering the calamities of natural disasters. During those years Clara Barton *was* the Red Cross, and the Red Cross was Clara Barton.

However, it was a situation that could not last forever, and in the end she was bound to have her heart broken. In 1898, at the age of 77, Barton once again took herself to the battlefields, this time in Cuba during the Spanish-American War. It was a memorably heroic act, but now inefficiencies were becoming apparent. The problem was not Barton's age—her daily activities showed the same vigor—but that the organization's structure was simply too small and outdated to meet the demands and goals that it had set for itself.

Critics now wanted Barton to relinquish control and allow the Red Cross to grow. But it was not in her temperament to do so. As the pressure grew both from outside and inside the organization, the fight often turned bitter. Barton *could* not let go. "When the people got hold onto the Red Cross they would be uncontrollable," she claimed. Her opponents accused her of being autocratic, capricious, and careless with the organization's finances.

Finally, the U.S. Senate conducted hearings, prompted by allegations that Barton was mishandling Red Cross funds. She was exonerated completely. But it was over. Too much had been said against her. Too much of her energy had been drained in the fight.

In 1904 Barton resigned. It was not a graceful exit—Clara Barton did not have that in her makeup. "The government I thought I loved, and loyally tried to serve," she wrote shortly after her departure, "has shut every door in my face." No longer associated with the Red Cross, she continued to work out of her home at Glen Echo. But her life was never the same. She wrote, read, gardened, and started a new organization, the National First Aid Society. At 85, she was still nursing indigent relatives whom she had taken into her home.

In 1912, at age 91, Barton died at Glen Echo. Just days before her death she apologized to her attending physicians for moaning in pain. It was one of the few apologies she ever felt cause to make.

Today Clara Barton's home in Glen Echo is a National Historic Site. Here the visitor can still feel the presence of a remarkable woman and the remarkable life she led. Scattered throughout the large house are small artifacts, photographs (one of her beloved cat, Tommy), portraits, books, a diary. But it becomes immediately obvious that Barton's personal life is not to be found in those homey reminders but instead in the all-pervasive presence of *her* organization, the American Red Cross. From the Red Cross

The doors off this upstairs hallway led to rooms where nurses often recuperated after the exhausting work of disaster relief. (American Red Cross)

windows gracing the front of the house and the many flags and Red Cross testimonials hanging from the hallways, to the original office doors marked American Association of the Red Cross and the large storage closets for relief supplies discreetly placed behind paneled walls, the visitor is reminded that for Clara Barton the Red Cross *was* her personal life.

Clara Barton's house at Glen Echo, Maryland also served as the headquarters for the American Red Cross. (Courtesy of the National Park Service)

Yet she also loved the house at Glen Echo. Her bedroom at the back of the house had a view of the Potomac River valley, and the place had a peaceful, rural atmosphere, with vegetable and flower gardens, chickens, horses, and cows. As a friend once recalled, "She loved her Glen Echo home, and used to say the moon seemed always to be shining there."

Typical of the complexly interwoven relationship between Clara Barton and the American Red Cross, Glen Echo was deeded directly to Barton even though it was understood that the house was Red Cross property. In 1909, weakened in her old age, and perhaps fearing that the Red Cross might try to reclaim the house after her death, Barton signed it over to an associate, Dr. Julian Hubble, who had helped supervise the construction of the building.

After Barton's death, Dr. Hubble and a few other associates formed the Clara Barton Association, hoping to turn the house into a monument to Barton's memory. Financing fell short of what was needed and the plan was about to be put on hold when a strange situation developed. Arriving on the scene was Mable Rawson Hirons, a native of North Oxford, Massachusetts and an acquaintance of Barton's and Hubble's. Hirons claimed that Barton's spirit had appeared to her at a séance and instructed her to take charge of the Glen Echo house. Barton herself had taken to attending séances in her old age and claimed to have spoken to the spirits of such long dead personages as Abraham Lincoln and General Ulysses S. Grant, so Dr. Hubble apparently accepted this mystical message, along with Hirons's claim that she had the funds to solve all of the association's financial problems. The doctor signed the house over to Hirons.

Unfortunately, it soon became apparent that Hirons was far from wealthy and was in fact paying off her debts by renting out rooms in the house and selling off the furniture. She also evicted the credulous Dr. Hubble, who was then abandoned by other members of the foundation who couldn't believe he had been foolish enough to let Hirons take over the house. Left with practically nothing, Hubble was taken in by some kindly neighbors who convinced him to sue for return of the deed. Four years later the courts finally returned the house to him.

After Dr. Hubble's death in 1929 the house was inherited by his two nieces, Rena and Lena Hubble. Lena moved into Glen Echo and turned it into a rooming house, which she ran until selling out to Josephine Frank Noyes in 1942. Mrs. Noyes and her sister continued to rent rooms for a number of years, promoting their property with an invitation to come and see "the house where Clara Barton lived." Fortunately for visitors today, Mrs. Noyes and her sister took good care of the original household furnishings and even went so far as to buy back some of the items sold off by Hirons. Upon Mrs. Noyes's death in 1958, her four sisters inherited the house. In 1963, the elderly sisters decided that the house was too big for them to manage and attempted to sell it. They were offered $50,000 by an amusement park that had opened up next door and wanted the lot for additional parking. Knowing that this would mean the destruction of the house, the sisters offered to sell it to anyone who could come up with at least $35,000 and would promise to save and maintain the property. It was a generous gesture that meant a financial loss to the sisters.

Understanding the situation, a group of Montgomery County Red Cross volunteers proposed that the American Red Cross purchase the house and preserve it as a historic site. The Red Cross answered that it could not use its funds for such a purpose. It did, however, lend its support to a preservation project. In May 1963, the organization urged all Red Cross volunteers to support the efforts of the Montgomery County group, now incorporated as

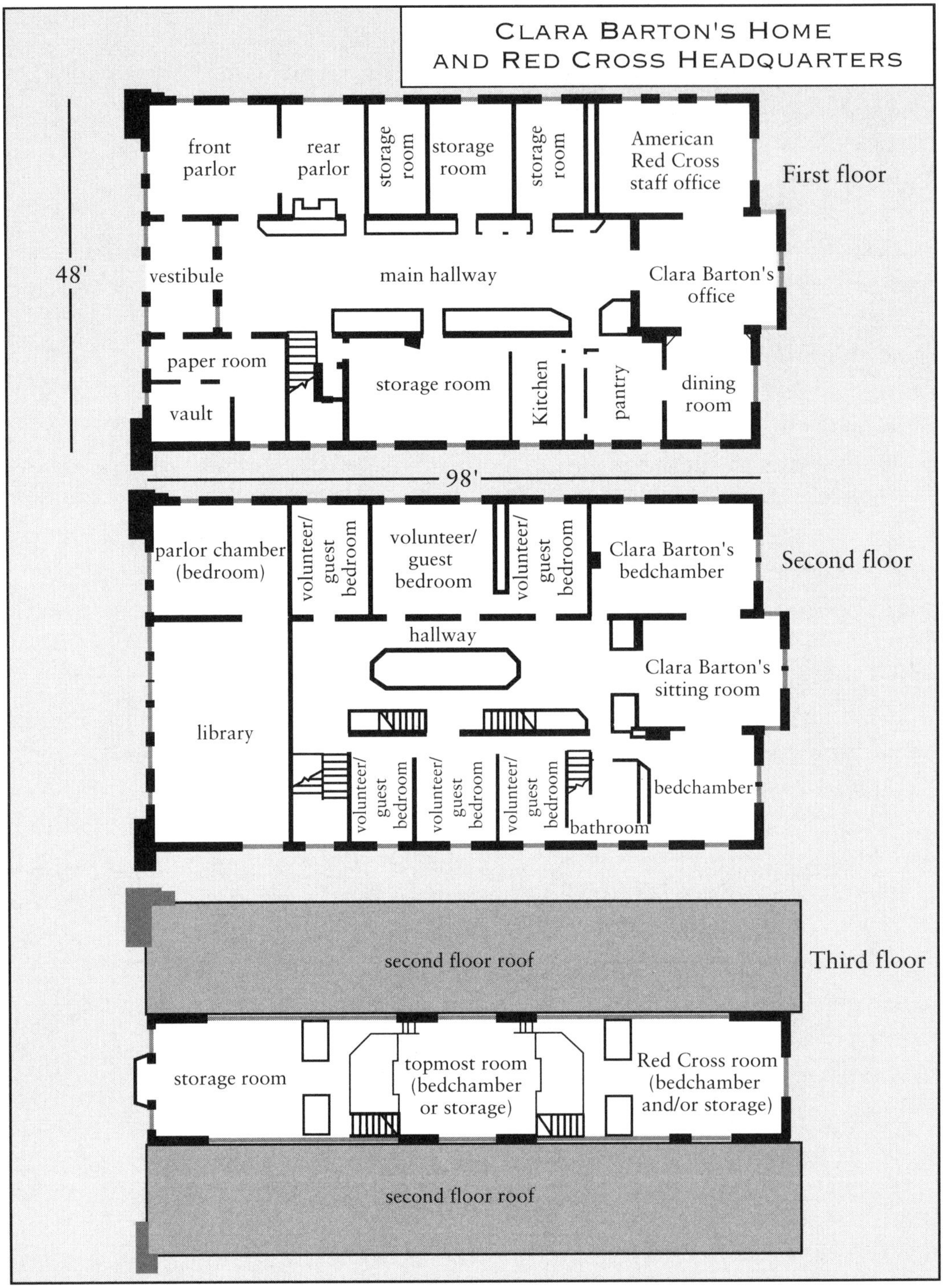
CLARA BARTON'S HOME
AND RED CROSS HEADQUARTERS
First floor
front parlor
rear parlor
storage room
storage room
storage room
American Red Cross staff office
vestibule
main hallway
Clara Barton's office
paper room
vault
storage room
Kitchen
pantry
dining room
48'
98'
Second floor
parlor chamber (bedroom)
volunteer/ guest bedroom
volunteer/ guest bedroom
volunteer/ guest bedroom
Clara Barton's bedchamber
hallway
Clara Barton's sitting room
library
volunteer/ guest bedroom
volunteer/ guest bedroom
volunteer/ guest bedroom
bathroom
bedchamber
Third floor
second floor roof
storage room
topmost room (bedchamber or storage)
Red Cross room (bedchamber and/or storage)
second floor roof

the Friends of Clara Barton. Through bake sales and a hodgepodge of other events, the group managed to raise the necessary funds, and on January 1, 1964 the sisters agreed to sell Glen Echo to the Friends of Clara Barton.

A CLOSE-UP — INNER CONFLICTS OF AN ANGEL

Clara Barton fought valiantly to bring shelter to the homeless, comfort to the wounded, and aid to the dying. Her position of high esteem in American history is unassailable. She reached beyond the constrictions placed on 19th-century women, defining herself not by the parameters of her home but by the needs of a larger world.

But Barton was a woman plagued with self-doubts. Maybe that's why she told stories of her own bravery—to bolster her flagging sense of self-worth. Feeling responsible for everything around her, she could never bring herself to delegate authority. She feared that no one else could or would do a task as well as she. As a result she often worked alone. Over and over she exhausted herself, bringing on nervous breakdowns and chronic ill health.

Barton was loyal to her friends and had a sense of humor that often surprised those around her. But she was also private and shy, even timid, and insecure. This side of her personality always remained in conflict with her resolute belief in the humanitarian causes she fought for. As she remarked in 1866, as the Civil War raged around her, "You must never so much as think whether you like it or not, whether it is bearable or not; you must never think of anything except the need, and how to meet it." An understanding of her personal conflicts sheds new light on the remarkable courage of this "angel of the battlefield."

Opposite: *Built in 1891, this three-story, 30-room house served both as American Red Cross headquarters and as Clara Barton's home. Storage rooms on the first floor provided space for supplies, and the several bedrooms on the second floor offered temporary housing for volunteers and guests.*

PRESERVING IT FOR THE FUTURE

In April 1965, the Clara Barton House was designated a National Landmark. The Friends of Clara Barton made their final payment on the mortgage in early 1975 and in April that same year they presented the deed to the house to the National Park Service. In December 1979 they disbanded their organization and donated their treasury—an additional $8,435.37—to help purchase additional furnishings for the house.

EXPLORING FURTHER

Books about Clara Barton

Bains, Rae. *Clara Barton, Angel of the Battlefield.* Mahwah, N.J.: Troll Associates, 1982.

Dubowsky, Cathy East. *Clara Barton: Healing the Wounds.* Englewood Cliffs, N.J.: Silver Burdett Press, 1991.

Hamilton, Leni. *Clara Barton.* New York: Chelsea House, 1987.

Oates, Stephen B. *A Woman of Valor: Clara Barton and the Civil War.* New York: Free Press, 1994.

Pryor, Elizabeth B. *Clara Barton: Professional Angel.* Philadelphia: University of Pennsylvania Press, 1987.

Whitelaw, Nancy. *Clara Barton: Civil War Nurse.* Springfield, N.J.: Enslow, 1997.

Related Places

The Fairfax Station Railroad Museum
11200 Fairfax Station Road
Fairfax Station, Virginia 22039
(703) 425-9225
Internet: http://www.fairfax-station.org

Fairfax Station, originally built by Irish immigrants during the railroad-building heyday of the 1850s, became a Civil War emergency treatment center during the summer of 1862. There, Clara Barton nursed soldiers injured in the bloody conflict—and earned her reputation as an angel of mercy. More than 3,000 wounded passed through this point, many getting treatment before being transported to Alexandria. Eventually destroyed by advancing Confederate soldiers, the station was later recaptured and rebuilt by the Union Army. It was closed in 1973, but concerned local residents began efforts to preserve the site in 1975, resulting in the construction of an exact replica of the original station. Today the building serves as both a museum of Civil War railroad history and a community center. The museum houses Civil War, Red Cross, and historic railroad memorabilia as well as a large variety of artifacts found in and around the original station.

Johnstown Flood National Memorial
P.O. Box 355
Saint Michael, PA 15951
(814) 495-4643

At 3:10 P.M., May 31, 1889, the South Fork Dam at Johnstown, Pennsylvania burst after a downpour of heavy rains, inundating the city. More than 2,200 people died on that tragic Friday, and thousands more were injured. The Johnstown Flood ranks as one of the worst disasters in American history. Clara Barton and 50 Red Cross workers provided aid to the injured and homeless. It was the first large-scale disaster to test the fledgling organization, and they helped provide unprecedented nursing care, feeding stations, and mass shelters. The Johnstown Flood National Memorial is located in southwestern Pennsylvania, about 10 miles northeast of Johnstown. The park contains nearly 165 acres and preserves the remains of the South Fork Dam and portions of the former Lake Conemaugh bed. (During the 1930s, the federal government rechanneled the Conemaugh River to provide better flood control.)

Wounded Knee

MONUMENT TO A LOST WAY OF LIFE
Pine Ridge, South Dakota

AT A GLANCE

Date: Wounded Knee Massacre, 1890;
American Indian Movement (AIM) demonstration, 1973.

Monument commemorating the massacre at Wounded Knee

The location of one of the most important and tragic events in American Indian–United States relations, this wind-swept, hilly spot, with its nearby ravine, is sacred ground to the Lakota (Sioux) who live here and to many other Indian peoples. It is the site of the last violent confrontation of the Indian Wars, and some 250 Native Americans lost their lives here.

Address:
Badlands National Park
(for information) Journey to Wounded Knee
P.O. Box 6
Interior, SD 57750
(605) 433-5361
Internet:http://www.nps.gov/badl

Pine Ridge Reservation
Off U.S. Route 18, Pine Ridge, SD 57770

At Wounded Knee Creek on December 29, 1890, nearly 500 well-armed troopers of the U.S. 7th Cavalry, some equipped with Hotchkiss guns—early versions of the modern machine gun—massacred an estimated 250 (out of some 350) Sioux men, women, and children in a South Dakota encampment. The army lost 25 men, mostly to their own stray bullets.

A people's dream died there. It was a beautiful dream. . . .
The nation's hoop is broken and scattered. There is no
center any longer, and the sacred tree is dead.

—Black Elk, Oglala Sioux

♦♦♦♦♦

A Lakota encampment, Pine Ridge, South Dakota, 1891 (Nebraska State Historical Society)

It was an exhausted band of Miniconjou Sioux—led by Big Foot, their ailing and aged chief—who arrived in the hilly regions of the Pine Ridge Indian Reservation in December 1890. They had been fleeing for hundreds of miles, driven by fear, and many of the band of 120 men and 230 women and children were weakened by their ordeal. Some traveled on ponies. Others rode in decrepit wagons or walked wearily beside their travois, frameworks made of long poles constructed to carry baggage behind their horses.

Meanwhile, American soldiers were searching for them; the generals were convinced that the Miniconjou and others who practiced the Ghost Dance religion in the South Dakota region were planning attacks against white settlers in the area. The government had banned the Ghost Dance, thinking that it was a potential source of trouble, and was intent on arresting anyone who continued practicing the rituals of that religion.

The stage for confrontation had been set, completely without intention, by a Northern Paiute holy man named Wovoka, whose Ghost Dance religion promised that a brighter future awaited the Indians and that by performing the Ghost Dance, they could help bring it about. Wovoka's wisdom came to him in a vision that occurred during an eclipse of the sun on New Year's Day 1889. "When the Sun died," he said, "I went up to heaven and saw God and all the people who had died a long time ago. God told me to come back and tell my people they must be good and love one another, and not fight or steal, or lie. He gave me this dance to give my people." As the mythology evolved and spread to other tribes, those who followed the Ghost Dance religion said there would be a new era in the future, when all those who had died would return and there would be no white people. Some versions of this religion held that garments worn during the dance, called Ghost Shirts, would also make the wearer impervious to enemy bullets. The new religion gave hope to many Indians all over the country, some of whom traveled as delegates to Wovoka's conferences, returning with renewed inspiration and fervor to practitioners on the reservations.

U.S. government officials were disturbed by these activities and began building up military installations near reservations, in case trouble erupted. During this time, a group of the Lakota people, who lived in South Dakota, had started to practice the Ghost Dance. On the Cheyenne River Sioux Reservation, the government had ordered Chief Big Foot's arrest for his support of the dance, although Big Foot no longer practiced the ritual. He and his band of 350 fled their village and crossed 150 miles of plains and badlands through ice storms and snow. They hoped to find safety on the Pine Ridge Reservation, where they might be protected by the strength of the Oglala Sioux led by Chief Red Cloud, who had extended an invitation to them.

During the journey, Big Foot caught pneumonia. Wrapped in an overcoat, blood dripping from his nose, he rode in a horse-drawn wagon. His followers knew he was dying. They evaded capture at first, but the army rounded them up on the Pine Ridge Reservation on December 28, 1890 and escorted them to the military camp near Wounded Knee Creek. The next morning the cavalry commander, Colonel James W. Forsyth, called a council to collect the band's weapons. Accounts vary about what happened next, but according to many, the Lakota, surrounded by cavalry and infantry, reluctantly surrendered their arms. A few young warriors tried to hide some weapons beneath their blankets as they stood in the council circle. When pressed, they too relinquished their guns, except for one, who brandished his rifle in the air. A shot went off. The troops unleashed a tremendous barrage of rifle and machine-gun fire. Many Indians were killed instantly, and others were mowed down as they tried to escape to a nearby ravine. In the end, more than 200 Lakota men, women, and children lay dead. Twenty-five soldiers also lost their lives—mostly due to crossfire.

Later, a small group made their way to the snow-covered terrain to find and bury the dead. According to the account of Dr. Charles A. Eastman, the agency physician at Pine Ridge (of Santee Sioux heritage) who accompanied the party:

> Fully three miles from the scene of the massacre we found the body of a woman completely covered with a blanket of snow, and from this point we found them scattered along as they had been relentlessly hunted down and slaughtered while fleeing for their lives. . . . When we reached the spot where the Indian camp had stood, among the fragments of burned tents and other belongings we saw the frozen bodies lying close together or piled one upon another.

Along with those tragically killed that day, the promise of the Ghost Dance died for the Lakota people, and they were forced to accept reservation life.

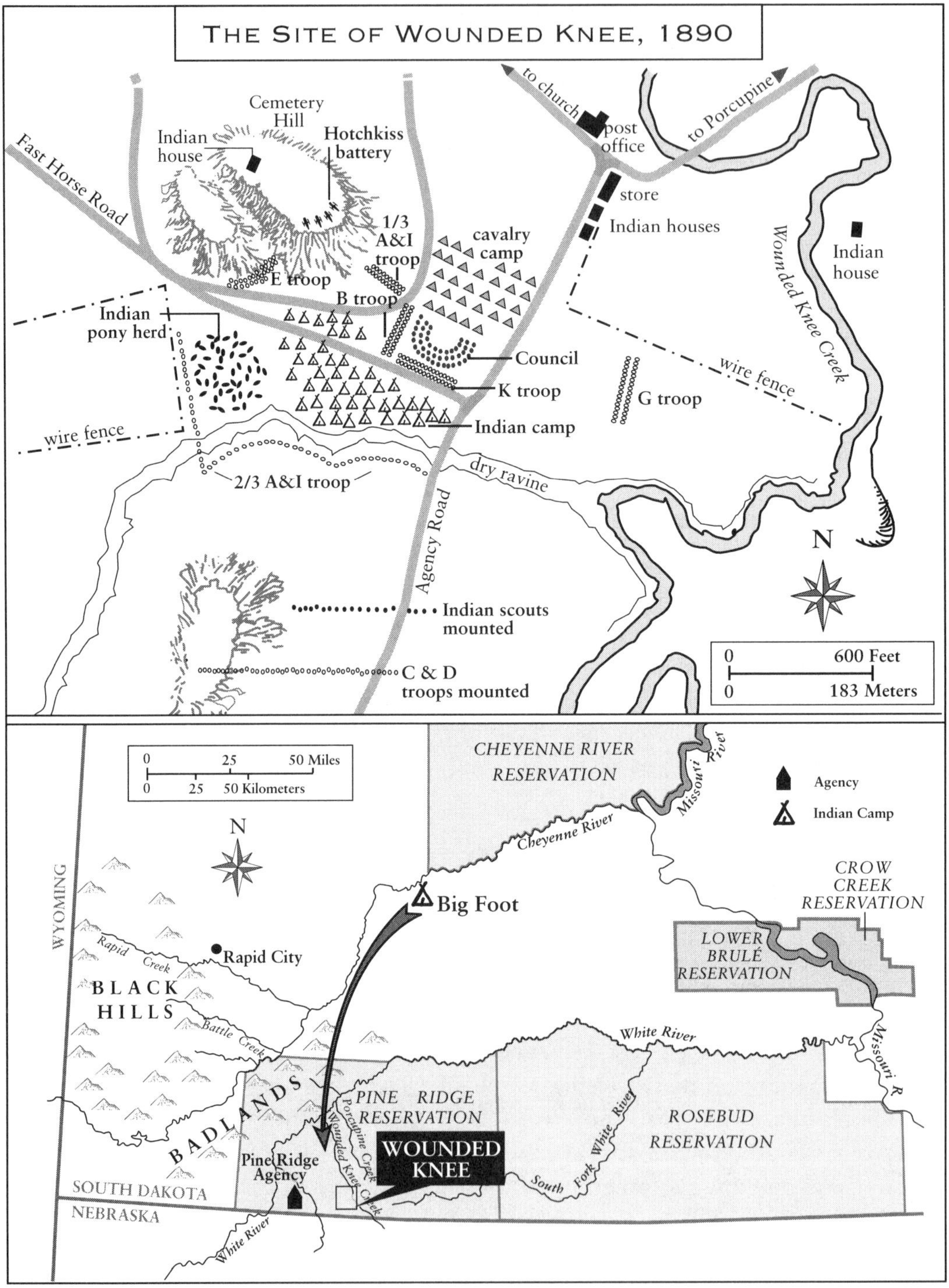
THE SITE OF WOUNDED KNEE, 1890
to church
post office
to Porcupine
Cemetery Hill
Indian house
Hotchkiss battery
Fast Horse Road
store
Indian houses
Wounded Knee Creek
Indian house
1/3 A&I troop
cavalry camp
E troop
B troop
Indian pony herd
Council
K troop
G troop
wire fence
Indian camp
wire fence
2/3 A&I troop
dry ravine
Agency Road
N
Indian scouts mounted
C & D troops mounted
0 600 Feet
0 183 Meters
0 25 50 Miles
0 25 50 Kilometers
CHEYENNE RIVER RESERVATION
Missouri River
Agency
Indian Camp
Cheyenne River
N
WYOMING
Big Foot
CROW CREEK RESERVATION
Rapid City
Rapid Creek
LOWER BRULÉ RESERVATION
BLACK HILLS
Battle Creek
White River
Missouri R.
BADLANDS
PINE RIDGE RESERVATION
Porcupine Creek
White River
ROSEBUD RESERVATION
Pine Ridge Agency
Wounded Knee Creek
WOUNDED KNEE
South Fork White River
SOUTH DAKOTA
NEBRASKA
White River

The grim aftermath of the massacre of Wounded Knee (Nebraska State Historical Society)

For the United States, it was the end of the Indian Wars. The Lakota say that the sacred hoop of their nation—which they equate with the nation's life and health—broke at Wounded Knee.

But many Indians feel it need not remain broken. The story of Wounded Knee doesn't end in 1890. In 1968, young Indian activists formed a group called the American Indian Movement (AIM), which became the spearhead of the American Indian civil rights movement. A series of dramatic demonstrations called national attention to ongoing injustices against Indians: beginning in 1969, a 19-month occupation of an abandoned federal prison on Alcatraz Island in San Francisco Bay; a brief takeover of the Bureau of Indian Affairs offices in Washington, D.C. in 1972; and a 69-day occupation of the site of Wounded Knee in May 1973 by 200 members of AIM. With this action, Wounded Knee became a symbol of resistance and hope to the Indian Movement.

As a result of these initiatives, the official government policy of "termination" of Indian tribes was ended. The two-decade termination policy had discontinued legal recognition of tribes as sovereign bodies, and in some cases had

Opposite: *The top map shows the positions of* U.S. *military forces surrounding* Big Foot's *band (the council semicircle and tipis at the center of the map) at the time violence broke out at* Wounded Knee *on* December 29, 1890. *The bottom map shows the route taken by* Big Foot's *band across* South Dakota *to* Wounded Knee Creek *on the* Pine Ridge Reservation.

canceled many of their rights. But now, in response to AIM's pressure, the U.S. government embraced a new policy of Indian self-determination. In fact, as early as 1970, AIM's demonstrations were effecting policy changes. For example, in July of that year President Richard Nixon agreed to support the return of Blue Lake and 48,000 acres of land to the Indians of the Taos area. Lands near Davis, California became the home of a Native American university, and several others have since been founded. Native Americans now work in the federal Bureau of Indian Affairs, which has long played a key role in their day-to-day lives—but over which they never before had any influence.

The memory of Wounded Knee produced great bitterness and sorrow in the hearts of Indians throughout the United States, reflected in the words of Alex White Plume, a young Lakota, who spoke of the deep wounds that were still unhealed in the 1990s: "As Lakota people, we've only had contact with the white world for 163 years, that's all. . . . And we have not yet developed a ritual to forgive the white man for what he did. . . . He can't just come out here and apologize. First he has to 'wipe the tears of our nation.'"

In 1990, a century after the tragedy at Wounded Knee, the Lakota people of South Dakota and Native Americans throughout the country took the opportunity to honor those who died at Wounded Knee and to observe its symbolism for all American Indians. Many also expressed their wish for a mending process and a celebration of their unique culture, resolved to mend their sacred hoop, the Lakota Nation's traditional perception of identity, unity, and being in the integrated universe.

A CLOSE-UP: SURVIVORS OF WOUNDED KNEE

Of the some 350 people in Big Foot's band, few escaped with their lives. Marie Not Help Him, a Miniconjou Sioux and the granddaughter of one survivor, recalled her grandfather's memories: "And when Grandpa Beard used to tell it, he would say that the Wounded Knee Massacre was very, very tragic. And he would say, if only they had just killed us men and left the women and the children, he said it would be good. And as he would speak, he would call out the names of the men, the first six men that were killed. It was like a roll call. The first six men that were killed under the white flag of truce were Big Foot, Spotted Thunder, Horn Cloud, Ghost Horse, Iron Eyes, Wounded Hand. It was like a roll call. . . . And if we don't tell it now, then it'll be lost. And if we don't teach our children, then that too will be lost."

Newspaper correspondent Thomas H. Tibbles of the Omaha *World-Herald* corroborated the Miniconjou accounts. "Though the active attack lasted perhaps twenty minutes," he wrote, "the firing continued for an hour or two, wherever a soldier saw a sign of life. Indian women and children fled into the ravine to the south, and some of them on up out of it across the prairie, but soldiers followed them and shot them down mercilessly."

Blizzard conditions made retrieval of the dead bodies impossible for three days, and when parties returned to bury the dead, they were

Blue Whirlwind (standing), a survivor of Wounded Knee, said she received 14 wounds. Two of her sons were also wounded, and her husband, Spotted Thunder, was killed. This photo was taken in spring 1891. (Nebraska State Historical Society)

sickened by the sight of the frozen bodies of women and children strewn in the snow.

Oglala holy man Black Elk, present at Pine Ridge in 1890, later said:

> I did not know how much was ended. When I look back now from this high hill of my old age, I can still see the butchered women and children lying heaped and scattered along the crooked gulch as plain as when I saw them with eyes still young. And I can see that something else died there in the bloody mud, and was buried in the blizzard. A people's dream died there. It was a beautiful dream. . . . The nation's hoop is broken and scattered. There is no center any longer, and the sacred tree is dead.

PRESERVING IT FOR THE FUTURE

Today only a sign and mass grave mark the site of the Wounded Knee Massacre on South Dakota's Pine Ridge Indian Reservation. But visitors to Wounded Knee can view the creek, the grass-covered hills, and the ravine where the massacre occurred and they can contemplate the meaning of the place. They can also sense the sacredness of the site to the Lakota people, many of whom view the entire area as a burial ground. Nearby Badlands National Park can supply directions and a map that helps visitors visualize the scene just prior to the massacre of December 29, 1890.

EXPLORING FURTHER

Books about Wounded Knee and the American Indian Movement

Brown, Dee Alexander. *Bury My Heart at Wounded Knee.* New York: Washington Square Press, 1981.

Ehrlich, Amy. *Wounded Knee: An Indian History of the American West.* Adapted for young readers from Dee Brown's *Bury My Heart at Wounded Knee.* New York: Holt, Rinehart and Winston, 1974.

Jensen, Richard E., et al. *Eyewitness at Wounded Knee*. Great Plains Photography Series. Lincoln, Neb.: University of Nebraska Press, 1991.

Neihardt, John G. *Black Elk Speaks: Being the Life Story of a Holy Man of the Oglala Sioux*. Paperback ed. Lincoln, Neb.: University of Nebraska Press, 1988.

Smith, Paul Chaat, and Robert Allen Warrior. *Like a Hurricane: The Indian Movement from Alcatraz to Wounded Knee*. New York: The New Press, 1996.

Related Places

The Heritage Center
Red Cloud Indian School
P.O. Box 100
Pine Ridge, SD 57770
Phone: (605) 867-5491
Fax: (605) 867-1291
Internet:http://www.redcloudschool.com

Within the Heritage Center located on the Pine Ridge Reservation, the Museum of Native American Fine Arts has an excellent collection of paintings, sculpture, Lakota star quilts, and Lakota artifacts. The Red Cloud Indian Art Show takes place yearly from the first Sunday of June until the second Sunday of August.

Badlands National Park
P.O. Box 6
Interior, SD 57750
(605) 433-5361
Internet: http://www.hps.gov/badl

Located adjacent to the Pine Ridge Indian Reservation in southwestern South Dakota, Badlands National Park extends over nearly 244,000 acres, preserving the stark beauty of lands the Plains Indians once called home. Here the Badlands' eroded land formations jut against the sky in the form of buttes, pinnacles, and spires. The park also contains the largest protected mixedgrass prairie in the United States and 64,000 acres of wilderness. The National Park Service co-manages the Stronghold Unit of the park with the Oglala Lakota (Sioux) tribe, preserving the sites of the Ghost Dances of 1890. While preserving some 11,000 years of human history, Badlands National Park also contains a fossilized record of life dating back 23 to 35 million years—the richest fossil beds from the Oligocene epoch in the world.

Ellis Island Immigration Center

GATEWAY TO AMERICA
Liberty Island, New York

AT A GLANCE

Built: Original pine building, 1892; current Main Building, 1900; most additional buildings, 1900–15

Central processing center for immigrants 1892–1924; detention center, 1924–54.

Located on an island near the Statue of Liberty in New York Harbor, these brick Byzantine and French Renaissance buildings were used as a processing center for millions of immigrants, primarily from Europe, who entered the country in the early 20th century.

Address:
Statue of Liberty National Monument and Ellis Island
Liberty Island
New York, NY 10004
Telephone: (212) 363-3200
Fax: (212) 363-8347
Internet: http://www.nps.gov/stli
http://www.ellisisland.org
E-mail:stli_ museum@nps.gov

Millions of people, attracted by the promise of a better life, streamed to American shores between 1892 and 1924. For those disembarking from ships landing in New York Harbor, Ellis Island was their first taste of life in America. Nearly one out of every two Americans today has an ancestor who came through Ellis Island.

Give me your tired, your poor, . . . your huddled masses
yearning to breathe free . . .

—From a poem by Emma Lazarus inscribed on the pedestal of the Statue of Liberty

♦♦♦♦♦

There are empty benches lining the walls of the sprawling room with the Spanish tile floor. Scattered about forlornly are the once-busy wooden tables used by the inspectors. Looking out some of the huge windows you can see the majestic figure of the Statue of Liberty standing proudly nearby. Time, it seems, has stopped inside this huge building, on this small island. But the ghosts and the memories of the past linger.

The view one sees arriving at Ellis Island (Courtesy of the National Park Service)

The gigantic Great Hall is empty now, except for the tourists and the guides, their footsteps sometimes echoing in the vastness. Once, thousands of people were crowded here daily, in groups, in lines, and in constant bustling activity, their voices blending into an incredible din, speaking, shouting, laughing, and sometimes crying, in a dozen different languages and accents. On April 17, 1911, a one-day record was set: 11,745 immigrants passed through this hall. But that figure was not unusual. Each day for more than three decades, thousands came streaming in, hopefully, fearfully, anxiously, from the far corners of the world, seeking a new life, a better existence, a bright new dream in America. From 1892 until 1924 over 12 million immigrants were processed on Ellis Island, and today more than 40 percent of Americans, over 100 million people in all, can trace their roots back to an ancestor who passed through the Great Hall.

Situated in upper New York Harbor, about one mile southwest of the Battery in New York City and just off the waterfront of Jersey City, New Jersey, Ellis Island is within rowing distance of either shore. In the beginning it was just a few acres in size. Called Kioshk (Gull Island) by the local Indians, it was primarily known for its rich oyster beds. During the Dutch and English colonial periods it became known as Oyster Island but went through a dozen or so different names and uses before it was acquired by a New York City butcher named Samuel Ellis in 1785. Eventually New York State bought the island and then in 1808 sold it for $10,000 to the United States government, which used it as a fort and later as an ammunition depot before designating it as the site of the nation's largest immigration station in 1892.

Prior to 1890, individual states were responsible for regulating immigration into the United States. The immigration station for the State of New York, the country's busiest point of entry, occupied a building called Castle Garden, located at the Battery at the tip of Manhattan Island. But changing economic conditions, political instability, restrictive religious laws, and a sense of general unrest throughout Europe during the late 1800s had led to a great new influx. The largest human migration in the history of the world took place during this period. With most of these refugees arriving in the United States through the port of New York, Castle Garden was soon overwhelmed. Also, corruption had infiltrated the Castle Garden operation, and the federal government intervened by taking over the station's duties and building a new facility on its Ellis Island property.

The Ellis Island depot, which cost the federal government $500,000 to construct, opened its doors on January 1, 1892. Annie Moore, a 15-year-old girl from Ireland, was the first to pass through the doors, with her two younger brothers close behind her. To celebrate the occasion, the immigration commissioner for the port of New York gave Annie a ten-dollar gold piece.

The buildings, built of Georgia pine, had been hastily put together, and a disastrous fire five years later destroyed most of the structures, as well as most records. The new Ellis Island facility reopened on December 17, 1900, this time with the fireproof, redbrick buildings still standing today. Over the years, the island's size also expanded, from its original 3 acres to nearly 28, a transformation achieved primarily by the use of dumped ballast from ships and earth fill excavated during construction of the New York City subway system. On the first day of Ellis Island's reopening, over 2,000 immigrants passed through its doors.

What was it like to pass through Ellis Island—often the first footsteps on American soil for these tired, bewildered, and frightened new arrivals? You can hear many of their stories today by using the earphones set up throughout the exhibit areas, or in the special listening room on the third floor of this once-bustling complex that has become both a museum and a memorial. The taped reminiscences are part of the Oral History Project, which historians first began in 1973 and continue to expand today. The tapes allow you to hear the stories of hundreds of Ellis Island immigrants in their own voices.

You can also explore the buildings, tour dozens of exhibits in 30 galleries, and visit two theaters featuring the moving and award-winning film, *Island of Hope, Island of Tears*. You can view artifacts, including the actual baggage carried by some of these new arrivals, personal mementos, and historic photos. And you can stand in the Great Hall, more formally known as the Registration Room; here, where most of the island's activities took place, the echoes of the past complement the stories that have been preserved on tape.

Most of those stories begin in poverty and hope, for the people who passed through Ellis Island came with little money in their pockets. Those who had money, who could afford to pay for first- or second-class accommodations aboard ship, rarely set foot on Ellis Island. Officials assumed that anyone who had the means to travel first or second class would not become a medical or financial drain on the government. These arrivals were inspected and interviewed briefly, and in relative privacy, aboard the ships. Then they were free to walk down the gangplank and onto American soil.

But the third-class passengers and those traveling in steerage (economy quarters) found themselves quickly whisked off the ships and onto ferries or barges. With the great city of New York so near and yet so far away, after weeks of difficult shipboard travel, they were ferried to an island that looked much like a fortress, or a prison. Despite the redbrick of its French Renaissance Revival structures, a brooding, dismal air seemed to hover over the island in the early-morning fog.

There are horror stories about Ellis Island—no such place exists without them—and it's easy to imagine the fear and anxiety that must have gripped the hearts and minds of these newcomers to America's shores as they found themselves herded off the ferries, through the main doors, and into the Great Hall to be questioned and inspected. Efficient processing was the goal; there was little premium paid to human dignity. The vast majority of those arriving at the island were questioned, inspected, and free to go within three to five hours. But those hours were long, noisy, impersonal, intrusive, and for many both bewildering and frightening.

The first officials that the immigrants encountered on the island were federal physicians who searched through the crowds of arriving newcomers for signs of contagious diseases or obvious physical or mental abnormalities that might limit the newcomers' abilities to support themselves. Chalk marks were rubbed on the clothes of those suspected of harboring any deficiencies—an "E" for suspected eye problems, "H" for heart, "K" for hernia, "L" for lameness, and "X" for mental disorders. Those so marked would be held for more thorough examination.

The next stop for most was to the inspectors' tables in the Great Hall. There, groups of passengers would be herded together, waiting for their names to be called over the incredible din of the crowd. The inspectors' questions focused on marital status, occupation, nationality, final destination, and how much money each immigrant carried. Most of these questions were actually cross-examinations based on the immigrant's personal entries in the ship's manifest log, which had been filled out at their point of embarkation. Sometimes, if the inspectors were suspicious or the answers were evasive or at variance with the information in the log, the interrogation would be longer and more probing.

Inside the Great Hall hundreds of immigrants waited to be processed. (Courtesy of the National Park Service)

Those who passed the physical and verbal inspections received cards stamped with the word *Admitted* and were free to leave, taking a ferry back to Manhattan or a barge to the railroad piers of New Jersey. Before leaving they could exchange their money for American currency and purchase railroad tickets at booths on the island. Two-thirds of those admitted during the island's peak years bought train tickets for places other than New York City.

Not all, though, passed through Ellis Island so quickly. About one in six immigrants was detained longer than the usual three to five hours. Those held from entry on medical, financial, or other grounds received housing in the sprawling dormitories and medical facilities on the island, while the final disposition of their cases was determined. Sometimes the problems were solved within a few days. Money or assistance from relatives already in America could provide help for those arriving with too little to support themselves. And sometimes a cough that had seemed suspicious turned out to be nothing other than a simple cold.

Some of the hopeful immigrants, however, never set foot on another piece of American soil but were sent back to their countries of origin. Although only slightly more than 2 percent of all the arrivals at Ellis Island met such a fate, for those individuals—some 250,000 in all—the experience was heartbreaking. For that 2 percent Ellis Island earned the nickname the Island of Tears.

But for those millions who made it through, no matter what their destinations, or indeed, their future, Ellis Island was at the time of their arrival the Island of Hope, the start of a new beginning. Many would succeed in their dreams, and many would fail. Some who left the island with the prized *Admitted* cards in their hands would go on to become famous—among them, United States Supreme Court Justice Felix Frankfurter, science and science-fiction writer Isaac Asimov, comedian Bob Hope, song-writer Irving Berlin, film director Elia Kazan, and motion picture actors Bela Lugosi and Edward G. Robinson. Others included the great football coach Knute Rockne; Father Edward Flanagan, the founder of Boys Town; and Baron von Trapp and the Trapp family, whose story was made famous by the motion picture *The Sound of Music.*

Some would become infamous, drifting into the more shadowy aspects of American life. Most would become neither famous nor infamous. They would become average Americans, living average American lives, working, striving, building families and futures, continuing to dream dreams, large and small, sometimes realizing their ambitions and sometimes falling short. They would simply become a part of America, a nation made up of immigrants and a nation built brick by brick by immigrants.

It is to them, and in their memory that the Ellis Island Immigration Museum is dedicated, a constant reminder of the nation's immigrant history—the history of America itself.

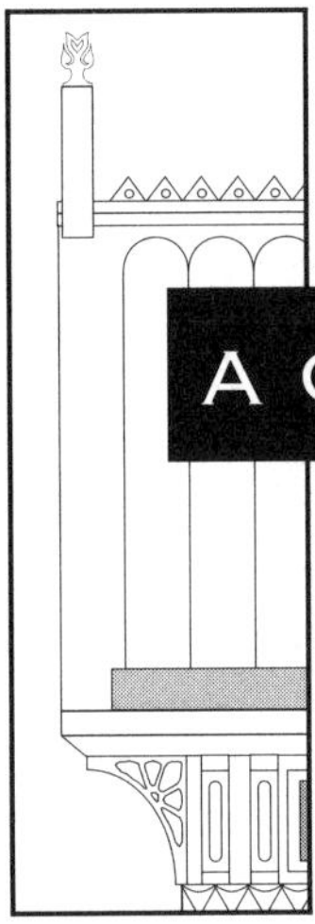

A CLOSE-UP

FREEDOM TO LAND IN A FREE LAND?

Not everyone who came to the United States between 1892 and 1924 went through processing at Ellis Island—but 12 million did. They were poor; in fact, many were penniless. But, as the *Jewish Daily Forward* pointed out in 1909, "They are the ones who have built the palaces, machines, food, and clothing which America enjoys today." They were craftsmen and intellectuals, farmers and laborers, tradespeople and merchants. Most were energetic and motivated. All were courageous, coming to a land they had never seen, whose language many didn't speak, and without a penny to return home if they didn't like it. Many found a better life. And they also contributed to the economic, cultural, and intellectual life of the country.

Every nation tries to control immigration, to strike a balance between the gains it can derive by admitting immigrants and the drain brought on by admitting too many people who can't support themselves, or might injure others. The inspectors at Ellis Island were charged with the difficult task of deciding who should be allowed to land in a free land.

Many of those who came through Ellis Island were young and frightened, and their recollections are poignant. "We were put on a barge, jammed in so tight that I couldn't turn 'round, there were so many of us, you see, and the stench was terrible," remembered a woman who emigrated from England as a young girl.

One man from France recalled, "I can remember standing in line with my mother, and being so short that I looked at people's legs much of the time. The eye exam stands out in my memory since it hurt." Many women came from cultures where they were unused to being touched by any man other than their husband, and the medical exam was especially traumatic for them (although a matron was always present).

Mental testing was less than scientific, and 9 out of 100 immigrants, according to a 1917 U.S. Public Health Service manual, were marked with

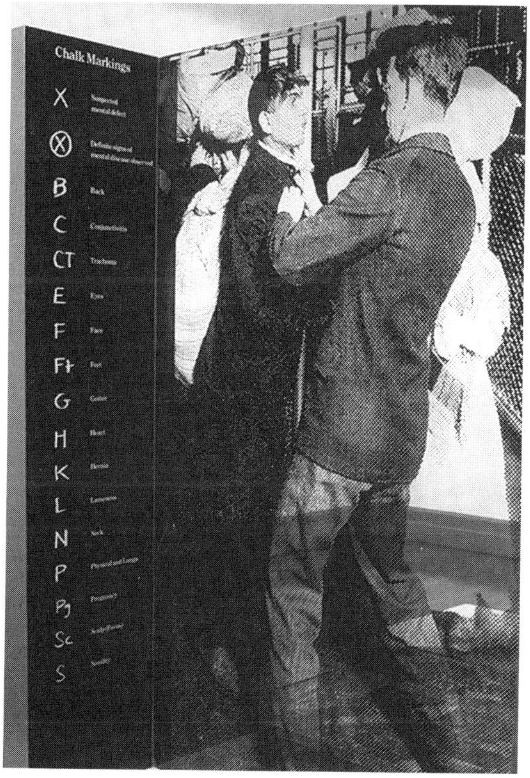

This exhibit at Ellis Island shows the chalk mark symbols used to separate immigrants into groups for further evaluation. (Courtesy of the National Park Service)

an *X* for further inspection. Pauline Notkoff, a Polish immigrant in 1917, recalled in 1985, "They asked questions. 'How much is two and one? How much is two and two?' But the next young girl also from our city, went and they asked her, 'How do you wash stairs, from the top or from the bottom?' She say, 'I don't go to America to wash stairs.'"

Some were detained—sometimes as many as 20 percent of the immigrants inspected were sent to detention areas for days or even weeks. Those who were ill were hospitalized. "The time I spent on Ellis Island, seemed like the longest waiting period for me because of the regimen," said one detainee years later. "Naturally there had to be a regimen. It was the only way that they could handle that many people. I realize that now in retrospect. But at the time it was a nightmare. . . . They weren't unkind, but you had no communication with the people who took care of you. . . . And you had no communication with the other people that were there because everybody was so full of fright."

Some aspects of the law remain controversial for their unfairness and bias. The 1891 Immigration Act specifically barred Chinese immigrants, along with "idiots, insane persons, paupers, or persons likely to become public charges, persons suffering from a loathsome or dangerous contagious disease, persons who have been convicted of a felony or other infamous crime or misdemeanor involving moral turpitude, polygamists . . ." In 1903, anarchists and prostitutes were added to the list, and in 1907, unaccompanied children under age 16 and anyone with tuberculosis were also added. By 1917, literacy was also required, and other Asians in addition to Chinese were excluded. After the Russian Revolution, the questions asked of immigrants became even more complex. Today's immigration laws continue to cause debate and disagreement.

One of the important topics raised by the museum at Ellis Island is the cluster of issues surrounding immigration law, not least of which is the question, Who should be free to land in the land of the free?

PRESERVING IT FOR THE FUTURE

After 1924, as the tide of immigration declined, Ellis Island was used mostly as a detention center and was closed completely on November 16, 1954. It was incorporated into the Statue of Liberty National Monument on May 11, 1965, and after a massive, privately funded $156 million restoration, the site was reopened to the public on September 10, 1990. The Main Building on Ellis Island is now a three-floor museum dedicated to the history of immigration and the important role the island played during the mass immigration periods of the late 19th and early 20th centuries.

Self-guided permanent exhibits in the museum explore various aspects of the immigration experience. For example, "Through America's Gate" takes the visitor step-by-step through a series of displays illustrating the stages of the immigrant inspection process. "Peak Immigration Years (1880–1924)" covers the journey of immigrants to America and shows where they settled throughout the United States. "Treasures from Home" contains a touching display of personal objects and stories of arriving immigrants. And "The Peopling of America" offers a look at immigration trends, using statistics, timelines, and graphs.

The museum's research library contains materials related to the Statue of Liberty, Ellis Island, and immigration history, along with the Oral History Collection. It is open to the public.

Liberty and Ellis islands are accessible only by Statue of Liberty/Ellis Island Ferry, Inc. ferries, and one round-trip ticket covers visits to both islands. Ferries depart from Battery Park in New York and Liberty State Park in New Jersey.

EXPLORING FURTHER

Books about Ellis Island and the Immigrant Experience

Fisher, Leonard Everett. *Ellis Island: Gateway to the New World.* New York: Holiday House, 1986.

Kotker, Norman, Shirley C. Burden, et al. *Ellis Island: Echoes from a Nation's Past.* Edited by Susan Jonas. New York: Aperture Foundation, 1989.

Reef, Catherine. *Ellis Island.* Places in American History. New York: Dillon Press, 1991.

Reeves, Pamela. *Ellis Island: Gateway to the American Dream.* New York: Crescent Books, 1991.

Related Places

The Statue of Liberty
Statue of Liberty National Monument and Ellis Island
Liberty Island
New York, NY 10004
(212) 269-5755
Internet: http://www.nps.gov/stli
E-mail: stli_ museum@nps.gov

Located in upper New York Bay, the Statue of Liberty National Monument is administered together with nearby Ellis Island. The statue was designed by French sculptor F. A. Bartholdi and presented to the United States by the Franco-American Union to commemorate the principles of the American Revolution. Visitors can climb 354 steps (22 stories) to the crown of the 152-foot-tall statue, which dominates New York Harbor and has become a symbol of freedom throughout the world. Dedicated in 1886, it became a national monument in 1924 and was extensively restored in 1986.

Angel Island State Park
P.O. Box 318
Tiburon, CA 94920
(415) 435-1915 or 435-5390

Accessible only by ferry.
Ferry information: (415) 546-2896

Known as the Ellis Island of the West, Angel Island served as a western point of entry to the United States for many immigrants from 1910 to 1940. Originally built to enforce the Chinese Exclusion Act, passed in 1882, Angel Island also served as a prison for hundreds of Chinese immigrants (no other national group was singled out in this way). There, detainees were isolated from their families and interrogated. The average stay on Angel Island was two weeks, but some detainees were kept there as long as 22 months. The Angel Island Immigration Station was closed in 1940, and the Exclusion Act was finally repealed in 1943. Interpretive services on the island are provided by state park volunteers who are present at the historic sites on the island on Saturdays, Sundays, and holidays from May through October. The volunteers also conduct special tours for schools, clubs, and other groups. For more information, call (415) 435-3522.

The Civil Rights Movement

"CREATED EQUAL," TREATED UNEQUALLY
Montgomery, Birmingham, and Selma, Alabama

AT A GLANCE

Dates: 1955–64

Sites where African Americans defended the cause of equal rights for all

In the 1950s and 1960s, the eyes of the world turned to the United States as African Americans began to find a cohesive voice for denouncing injustices against blacks. The organized civil rights movement succeeded in bringing about change through the great courage and sacrifice of many individuals in many parts of the country. At the end of this chapter you'll find descriptions of places commemorating the determined spirit of reform that infused this movement.

"We shall overcome" were the watchwords of the civil rights movement of the 1950s and 1960s. No longer willing to accept de facto second-class citizenship, African Americans created the model for civil rights reform for an entire nation.

. . . when the history books are written in the future, somebody will have to say, 'There lived a race of people, black people . . . who had the moral courage to stand up for their rights.'

—Martin Luther King, Jr., Montgomery bus boycott

♦♦♦♦♦

Some historians say that the civil rights movement of the 1960s, like the Confederacy of the 1860s, began in Alabama. In a way, it did begin in Montgomery, Alabama. But it was a long time brewing, and before it was finished, it became a national cause that brought about deep changes in the country's political and social fabric and in the way the African-American community saw itself.

Progress after the Civil War may have seemed promising to abolitionists. Slavery came to an end, and in 1866 Congress passed a Civil Rights Act that gave citizenship to former slaves. The 14th Amendment to the Constitution accorded African Americans the right to vote, and the former Confederate states were forced to comply. African Americans had political power for the first time, and their vote helped put Republican Ulysses S. Grant in the White House. Many blacks were also elected to state legislatures.

But the African-American struggle was far from over. Angry, Southern whites organized the Ku Klux Klan, a secret organization whose members terrorized and murdered African Americans who sought to exercise their rights. They intimidated African Americans from voting in an attempt to regain exclusive political power.

In 1876, Rutherford B. Hayes, seeking votes during his presidential campaign, promised Southern whites he would support their "states' rights"

The Dexter Avenue Baptist Church in Montgomery, Alabama became the base of operations for the Montgomery bus boycott. (Courtesy of the Alabama Bureau of Tourism and Travel)

position. Once in office, he withdrew federal troops from the South, bringing the progressive Reconstruction era to an end. Soon most Southern states established "Jim Crow" laws, which sanctioned discrimination and segregation—a move bolstered by a series of Supreme Court decisions in the 1880s and 1890s.

Soon, throughout the South, separate facilities were the rule for everything from taxicab stands and drinking fountains to libraries and post offices. The Red Cross even kept segregated blood banks until the 1940s. Jim Crow laws couldn't re-institute slavery, but they did make African Americans into second-class citizens, relegated to the back door of virtually every establishment they entered.

African Americans had to put up with the indignities of "separate but equal" facilities of nearly every kind. For example, schools and public restrooms were only available to blacks if they were labeled *colored only.* Black residential areas became isolated as ghettos, and African Americans were not allowed to live anywhere else.

The bus system in Montgomery required black passengers to pay at the front of the bus and then get off and re-enter by the rear door to sit in the back—the only area where they were allowed to ride. White bus drivers often would drive away before a paid passenger could make it to the rear door. When the bus was full, if a white passenger needed a seat, any black passenger could be required to stand.

Though deeply unjust, the system was law. Finally, African Americans began to resist and organize. And on December 1, 1955, a slender black seamstress named Rosa Parks boarded a bus in Montgomery, Alabama, sat down, and then refused to give up her seat to a white man. A police officer boarded the bus and arrested her. Parks's action made headlines across the nation and touched off a bus boycott by the entire Montgomery black community, led by Martin Luther King, Jr.

After her arrest, Rosa Parks lost her job in the department store where she had worked as a seamstress. Her husband, a barber, was told not to discuss the boycott or mention Rosa's name to customers. Consequently he left his job, stating that he would not work in a shop where his wife's name was unwelcome.

The bus boycott was in many ways harder on the boycotters than on the income of the Montgomery transit lines. Boycotters still needed to get to work, to doctors, to stores, and to post offices. But now they had no way to get there. Churches, under Rev. King's leadership, set up taxi and bus services, and individuals volunteered the use of their cars. Many people walked to places they would otherwise have reached by bus.

It took a full year to win the struggle, but the boycotters did not give up. Despite having his house bombed in January 1956, King, too, did not give up; he continued to lead the boycott, emulating the passive resistance techniques used so successfully by Mohandas K. Gandhi against British rule in India. Ultimately, the bus boycott forced the integration of Montgomery city buses. In November 1956, the U.S. Supreme Court ruled that Jim Crow laws, such as those Rosa Parks violated in Montgomery, were unconstitutional.

Inequality was everywhere in the 1950s, including the education system. Jim Crow laws called for "separate but equal" public schools for black children, which were nearly always inferior to whites-only schools. But on May 17, 1954, the U.S. Supreme Court handed down a landmark decision on *Brown v. the Board of Education*, declaring racial segregation unconstitutional in the public schools. A second Supreme Court ruling of May 31, 1955, stipulated that educational integration was to be achieved with "all deliberate speed." And in a third milestone decision, the Supreme Court also placed a ban on segregation in tax-supported colleges and universities.

In 1957, nine black teenagers set out to demand compliance with the new rulings. They tried to register at Central High School in Little Rock, Arkansas, then an all-white school. The governor of Arkansas attempted to block them from admittance, posting state National Guard troops in front of the school. The students finally entered by means of a special Supreme Court edict, a presidential proclamation, and the protection of the 101st Army Airborne Division and a special federalized state militia. At last, after 80 years of Jim Crow laws, some real progress was afoot. In 1962, James Meredith enrolled in the University of Mississippi, paving the way for other black students to enter state universities throughout the South.

A new fervor and belief in equality and freedom began to grow among black and white Americans in the 1960s—much as it had a century before during the formation of the abolition movement, among Levi and Catharine Coffin's contemporaries. This movement was led by Martin Luther King, Jr. Following the nonviolent tactics of Gandhi, King led boycotts and mass marches to raise consciousness and demonstrate for the establishment of more just practices. His success encouraged others to demonstrate for their rights across the South. In 1957, the Southern Christian Leadership Conference (SCLC) formed in Atlanta to coordinate civil rights efforts, and King was elected president.

In 1960, a group of students who were denied service at a lunch counter in Greensboro, North Carolina staged the first sit-in for civil rights. King supported other sit-ins throughout the South, encouraged "freedom riders" to challenge segregation on interstate buses in 1961, and plunged into a major antisegregation campaign in Birmingham, Alabama in 1963. In Birmingham, he met with stiff opposition from police chief Eugene "Bull" Connor, who used police dogs and high-pressure water hoses to disperse the demonstrators. King was arrested and spent eight days in jail, during which time he wrote his famous "Letters from a Birmingham Jail," admonishing those who had counseled him to back off.

On August 28, 1963, 250,000 African Americans marched through the summer heat into Washington, D.C. in a dramatic protest against the status quo. Called the March on Washington for Jobs and Freedom, the event was organized through the coordinated efforts of several civil rights groups. In the nation's capital, in front of the Lincoln Memorial, Martin Luther King gave his now famous "I have a dream . . ." speech, in which he eloquently exhorted the people of the United States to share his vision of a time when all Americans would be judged on the basis of character, not color.

In 1965, King led a voter registration campaign in Alabama and a freedom march from Selma to Montgomery. These activities were fraught with danger. Segregationists saw every march, every boycott as another affront. But King and his followers believed in the righteousness—and the necessity—of their cause. "This is no time to engage in the luxury of cooling off or to take the tranquilizing drug of gradualism," said King on August 28, 1963. "Now is the time to make real the promises of democracy. Now is the time to make justice a reality for all of God's children." On April 4, 1968, this eloquent and dedicated worker on behalf of freedom and equality was cut down by an assassin's bullet in Memphis, Tennessee. King was only 39 years old.

But King left his dream behind as a legacy. He projected a new sense of worth and dignity to African Americans and poor people of all ethnic groups. His philosophy of nonviolent direct action and his strategies for social change

Reenactments of the historic Voting Rights March from Selma to Montgomery take place annually at the Edmund Pettus Bridge in Selma, Alabama. (Courtesy of the Alabama Bureau of Tourism and Travel)

through rational and nondestructive methods aroused the conscience of the nation to a level rarely achieved in history. Rev. King's wisdom, his words, his actions, his commitment, and his dreams are all intertwined with the American experience.

PRESERVING IT FOR THE FUTURE

In recent years, plaques have been erected in historic sites, museums have been built, and statues have been sculpted to commemorate the bravery of those who worked in the civil rights movement, those who took risks, and those who gave their lives. As one "foot soldier" of the movement put it, seeing these remembrances erected "helped us to be proud that we did not give in." The more effort we take to thoughtfully preserve this history, the more successful the country will be at continuing the dialogue on race relations that was begun by the civil rights movement. And that dialogue will help us to continue to grow. The people of Alabama, and of other states, have done a great deal toward respectfully preserving this part of our heritage, as shown in the following descriptions of sites. And in the coming years, interpretation will no doubt become even richer than it is now.

EXPLORING FURTHER

Books on the Civil Rights Movement

Allen, Zita. *Black Women Leaders of the Civil Rights Movement*. African-American Experience. New York: Franklin Watts, 1996.

Assensoh, A. B. *Rev. Dr. Martin Luther King, Jr., and America's Quest for Racial Integration*. Ilfracombe, Devon: Arthur H. Stockwell, 1987.

Branch, Taylor. *Parting the Waters: America and the King Years*. New York: Simon and Schuster, 1988.

Franklin, John Hope. *From Slavery to Freedom: A History of Negro Americans*. New York: Knopf, 1987.

Hull, Mary, and Nathan Irvin Huggins. *Rosa Parks*. Black Americans of Achievement. New York: Chelsea House, 1994.

Parks, Rosa, and Gregory J. Reed. *Quiet Strength: The Faith, the Hope, and the Heart of a Woman Who Changed a Nation*. Grand Rapids, Mich.: Zondervan Publishing House, 1995.

Williams, Juan. *Eyes on the Prize: America's Civil Rights Years, 1954–1965*. New York: Viking Press, 1986.

Related Places

Court Square and Rosa Parks Historical Marker
One Court Square
Montgomery, AL 36104

In this square, cotton and slave auctions once took place. Today, it bears a marker commemorating the afternoon of December 1, 1955, when Rosa Parks was arrested for refusing to give in to segregation. The Montgomery bus boycott arose from her determination. Ironically, a nearby marker stands on the site of the telegraph office from which the message was sent ordering the Confederate army to fire on Fort Sumter.

Dexter Avenue King Memorial Baptist Church
454 Dexter Avenue
Montgomery, AL 36104
(334) 263-3970

This church, where Martin Luther King, Jr. served as minister, was also his base during the Montgomery Bus Boycott of 1955–56. When the church was founded in 1887, whites in the community objected to the presence of an African-American church on such a prominent street. At various times in the past, including the boycott years, rocks thrown by angry mobs often smashed the windows. The original pews are still there, and so is the pulpit used by Rev. King. Today, a mural on the lower floor of the church depicts the journey King took as a civil rights leader, beginning with the Montgomery boycott and ending with his assassination in Memphis, Tennessee. Nearby you can see the Alabama State Capitol building and (directly across the street from the church) the Alabama Supreme Court, the two places where segregation laws were enacted and upheld.

Central High School
1500 Park Street
Little Rock, AR 72202
(501) 376-4751

In the fall of 1957, nine black students attempting to attend school here found themselves harassed and threatened by large crowds of angry whites. The governor of Arkansas used the state's National Guard to block the black youngsters from entering the building. Only through federal intervention did they succeed in making integration a reality as mandated by the Supreme Court decisions of 1954–55. Today, Central High School's students are mostly black, and on the school grounds visitors can see the historical marker recalling the events of 1957–58.

16th Street Baptist Church
Sixth Avenue and 16th Street North
Birmingham, AL 35203
(205) 251-9402
Internet: http://www.bham.net/bcri/sixtnth.html

This church became Birmingham headquarters for the civil rights movement, under the leadership of Dr. Martin Luther King, Jr. and Rev. Fred L. Shuttlesworth. Organized in 1873, the church has been at this site since 1884 and served as a center for Birmingham's African Americans during the days of the Jim Crow laws. Nearby Kelly-Ingram Park served as a gathering point for rallies and marches during the 1960s. A Ku Klux Klan bombing on September 15, 1963 took the lives of four African-American girls. Today, in

The 16th Street Baptist Church served as a focal point for the African-American community in Birmingham, Alabama. A Ku Klux Klan bombing took the lives of four black girls here in 1963. Many civil rights demonstrations of the 1960s began in nearby Kelly-Ingram Park. (Courtesy of the Alabama Bureau of Tourism and Travel)

the church's sanctuary, a stained-glass window of the crucified black Christ commemorates their martyrdom. (Admission by appointment.)

Kelley-Ingram Park
Fifth Avenue North at 16th Street
Birmingham, AL 35203

At this site, protestors gathered in the 1960s for marches to white neighborhoods in downtown Birmingham. Often blocked from leaving the park, they endured confrontations with the Birmingham police. Under orders from Public Safety Commissioner Bull Connor, the police used dogs and firehoses more than once against the demonstrators, many of whom were children and teenagers. Today, statues in the park recall these events and serve as a source of pride to people who participated, a remembrance that they did not give in and that they maintained their nonviolent tactics, even when violence was used against them and their children. Kelly-Ingram Park is central to the city's newly created civil rights district.

Birmingham Civil Rights Institute
520 Sixteenth Street North
Birmingham, AL 35203
(205) 328-9696
Internet: http://www.bham.net/bcri/index.html
E-mail: bcri.info@bcrimail.bham.lib.al.us

The Birmingham Civil Rights Institute, dedicated on November 15, 1992, functions as a multipurpose community center geared toward the promotion of research and human rights awareness locally and beyond. Programs, services, and exhibits offered by the institute serve to continue the commitment of the countless individuals who dared to confront racial discrimination and bigotry and to increase understanding among all people.

Edmund Pettus Bridge and Historical Marker
Highway 80
Selma, AL 36703

On Sunday, March 7, 1965, a group of demonstrators—most of them African-American—began marching from Selma to Montgomery, Alabama in a protest demanding voting rights for blacks. In an incident that was covered on nationwide television, mounted Alabama state troopers swooped down on the large but peaceful crowd, striking at demonstrators and riding down individuals amid stinging tear gas. One week later, President Lyndon Johnson proposed a Voting Rights Act to a special joint session of Congress. A historical marker recalls the encounter, and reenactments of the march take place here every year.

MORE PLACES TO VISIT

The chapters of this book explore only a few of the hundreds of historic sites that commemorate U.S. political and social movements. Following is a partial list of additional historical places that reflect the varied political and social history of the United States.

New England States

Norfolk County Courthouse
650 High Street
Dedham, MA 02026

This courthouse (built in 1827) was the scene of the Sacco-Vanzetti trial in 1920, symbolic of the controversy aroused by fear of communism in the post–World War I era.

Mid-Atlantic States

Hopewell Furnace National Historic Site
2 Mark Bird Lane
Elverson, PA 19520
Telephone: (610) 582-8773 (Voice); (610) 582-2093 (TDD)
Fax: (610) 582-2768

Hopewell Furnace was founded in 1771 by Mark Bird, the first ironmaster, and weapons for the Continental Army were manufactured here. It represents one of the finest examples of a rural American 19th-century iron plantation, with 14 restored structures open to the public, including a blast furnace, the ironmaster's mansion, and auxiliary structures. Interpretative programs demonstrate facets of ironmaking and rural life in the early 19th century.

Independence National Historic Park
313 Walnut Street
Philadelphia, PA 19106
(215) 597-8974 (visitor information)
(215) 597-1785 (TTY)
(215) 597-8787 administrative office

Packed with history, this 45-acre area in downtown Philadelphia includes many sites linked with the birth of the nation. Here stands the place, now known as Independence Hall, where the Declaration of Independence and the United States Constitution were signed. The Liberty Bell, which has become recognized internationally as a symbol of freedom, stands on display. Areas of the park evoke the time from 1790 to 1800, when Philadelphia was the capital of the United States, a city so populous and diverse that its history forms a sort of microcosm of early U.S. history. Visitors can also see where Benjamin Franklin's home once stood and learn about his life and his many scientific, philosophical, and political contributions to the young country's growth. About 20 buildings within the park area are open to the public.

Southeastern States

The Martin Luther King, Jr., National Historic Site
526 Auburn Avenue, NE
Atlanta, GA 30312
(404) 331-3920

This park of 52.3 acres includes the birthplace of Martin Luther King, Jr.; Ebenezer Baptist Church, where he, his father, and his grandfather preached; King's tomb; the community where he grew up; and several other sites of interest. The Martin Luther King, Jr., Center for Nonviolent Social Change is also located inside park boundaries.

Abraham Lincoln Birthplace National Historic Site
2995 Lincoln Farm Road
Hodgenville, KY 42748
(502) 358-3137

Established as a national park by Congress on July 17, 1916, this site commemorates the birthplace of Abraham Lincoln, who became the 16th president of the United States. Although the one-room log cabin where he was born is no longer standing, visitors can view a similar early 19th-century Kentucky cabin erected as a memorial and preserved inside the park museum. The park includes 116.5 acres of land, about one-third the acreage of the original "Sinking Spring Farm" settled by Thomas and Nancy Lincoln in fall of 1808. Their son Abraham was born there shortly afterward, on February 12, 1809.

Monticello
P.O. Box 316
Charlottesville, Virginia 22902
(804) 984-9822

Built 1770–89, Monticello was the home of Thomas Jefferson, a consummate statesman and philosopher, later the third president of the United States. Jefferson's interest in culture, art, and architecture is reflected in Monticello, which he designed, built, and maintained with great care.

Rhea County Courthouse
1475 Market Street
Dayton, Tennessee 37321
(423) 775-0361 (Dayton Chamber of Commerce, for visitor information)

This courthouse (built in 1890–91) was the scene of the controversial and widely publicized Scopes Monkey Trial of 1925, which highlighted the clash between fundamentalist and modernist thought in science, theology, philosophy, and politics. A museum in the courthouse basement commemorates the trial and is open weekdays. A reenactment based on trial transcripts takes place annually in July.

Gadsby's Tavern Museum
134 North Royal Street
Alexandria, VA 22314
(703) 838-4242

Among the best known of the 18th-century inns in colonial America, this site served as a meeting place for prominent leaders, including George Washington and Thomas Jefferson. Originally two taverns built side by side in 1770 and 1792, the place was named for the man who ran them, an Englishman named John Gadsby. Gadsby's establishment formed the center of much of Alexandria's social and political life in those early days, and today Gadsby's Tavern Museum, with its restored historic rooms, provides visitors with a glimpse of life in 18th-century Virginia.

Midwestern States

The Little White Schoolhouse
303 Blackburn Street
Ripon, WI 54971
(920) 748-6764 (Chamber of Commerce, site management)
Mailing Address:
P.O. Box 305
Ripon, WI 54971-0305

A key meeting took place here in 1854 (in conjunction with another meeting in Jackson, Michigan) to protest the extension of slavery, drawing dissatisfied Whigs, Free Soilers, and Democrats. These meetings were the first steps in a process that led to the formation of the Republican party. Open daily June through September, weekends in October and May, and by appointment during the winter.

Shaker Historical Museum
16740 South Park Boulevard
Shaker Heights, OH 44120
(216) 921-1201

The Shaker Historical Society established this museum in 1956 to exhibit Shaker furniture and relics gathered from the North Union Shaker community and other Shaker villages. The museum stands where three large Shaker dwellings formerly stood, at one time surrounded by an orchard and gardens, where the community raised apples and vegetables. A visit to the museum's impressive collection eloquently evokes the legacy of perfection, simplicity, utility, and durability left by the people who lived here.

Southwestern States

The Alamo
300 Alamo Plaza
San Antonio, TX 78205
(210) 225-1391

Built in 1718 as a Spanish mission, this site marks the 1836 battle between Santa Ana's Mexican troops and American defenders. In the fight for Texas independence, 189 American men lost their lives, including Colonel William Barret Travis, Jim Bowie, and Davy Crockett.

Western States

Manzanar National Historic Site
P.O. Box 426
Independence, CA 93526-0426
Telephone: (619) 878-2932 (Voice)
Fax: (619) 878-2949

Opened near Lone Pine, California in 1942, Manzanar was one of ten relocation centers where Japanese Americans and Japanese aliens were interned during World War II. Detainees were not accused of any crimes, nor did they receive hearings or trials. This site has been identified as the best preserved of the camps but has not been developed. Visitors can take a self-guided tour of the pagodalike police and sentry posts and the camp auditorium, and they can view the ruins of the administrative complex and other remains, including the camp cemetery. A tour booklet is available at the Interagency Visitor Center in Lone Pine (619) 876-6222 and at the Eastern California Museum in Independence (619) 878-0258.

MORE READING SOURCES

In addition to the suggested readings at the end of each chapter of this book, the following list provides additional suggestions for exploring further.

Chafe, William H. *The Road to Equality: American Women Since 1962*. The Young Oxford History of Women in the United States Series, vol. 10. New York: Oxford University Press, 1994.

Colman, Penny. *Strike! The Bitter Struggle of American Workers from Colonial Times to the Present (1824 to the Present)*. Brookfield, Conn.: Millbrook Press, 1995.

Farley, Karin Clafford. *Thomas Paine: Revolutionary Author*. American Troublemakers Series. Austin, Tex.: Raintree/Steck-Vaughn, 1992.

Gillenkirk, Jeff, and James Motlow. *Bitter Melon: Inside America's Last Rural Chinese Town*. Berkeley, Calif.: Heyday Books, 1993.

Reef, Catherine. *Monticello*. Places in American History. New York: Dillon, 1991.

Stanley, Jerry. *I Am an American: A True Story of Japanese Internment*. Paperback ed. New York: Crown, 1996.

———. *Big Annie of Calumet: A True Story of the Industrial Revolution*. Edited by S. Boughton. New York: Crown, 1996.

———. *Children of the Dust Bowl: The True Story of the School at Weedpatch Camp*. New York: Crown, 1994.

Valle, Isabel, *Fields of Toil: A Migrant Family's Journey*. Pullman: Washington State University Press, 1994.

Wagner, Shirley Ann. *Equality Now: Safeguarding Women's Rights*. Human Rights. Vero Beach, Fla.: Rourke Corp., 1992.

INDEX

Boldface page references indicate main headings. *Italic* page references indicate illustrations. The letter *m* following a page reference indicates a map or diagram.

D

E

F

G

H

I

J

K